ADVANCE PRAISE

"This inspiring and deeply personal book takes readers on a journey of self-discovery, healing, and empowerment. Through Sarah's honest reflections, we witness the struggle of reclaiming self-worth and the transformative power of finding her voice. It's a moving reminder that being heard is not just a right, but a powerful act of self-love."

—KIRAN MANN, CHIEF EXECUTIVE OFFICER, CONSOLIDATED GROUP OF BRAR'S

"Sarah has overcome adversity in her life personally and professionally to become a successful entrepreneur, spokesperson, and leader. This book, like its author, brings insight, energy, and empowerment to every reader. Sarah not only shares ideas with us but also has us believe that anything is possible."

—MARTY PARK, PRESIDENT, MASTER ENTREPRENEUR & MAGIC BEAN PLANTER, EVOLVE BUSINESS GROUP

"With authenticity, vulnerability, and the warmest humor, Sarah Barnes-Humphrey shares her path toward self-worth, inspiring us all to walk our own."

—JANE BORDEN, AUTHOR OF *CULTS LIKE US: WHY DOOMSDAY THINKING DRIVES AMERICA*

"Having had the pleasure of joining Sarah's podcast, Let's Talk Supply Chain, I have become inspired and motivated by Sarah's devotion to circularity. Sarah is the circular champion needed in this world of fast fashion and landfills. Blazing her way through the tough topic of supply chain, Sarah keeps it real while being interesting and captivating."

—SUTTON STRACKE, CO-FOUNDER, SUTTON BRANDS

"I Buried Her in a French Press is raw and unexpectedly funny. Sarah Barnes-Humphrey takes us on a journey of self-discovery with honesty and heart, proving that finding your voice starts with owning your story."

—SARAH DANDASHY, FOUNDER OF ASK A CONCIERGE, LUXURY TRAVEL AND HOSPITALITY AUTHOR, SPEAKER, AND TV PERSONALITY

"Resilience and self-worth walk hand in hand. Sarah shows us that when you honor your worth, the next best move always reveals itself. That's where growth begins."

—DAVE SANDERSON, PRESIDENT AND PUBLISHER OF *MOMENTS MATTER MAGAZINE*

I BURIED HER IN A FRENCH PRESS:
A MEMOIR ABOUT FINDING MY VOICE
AND THE POWER OF BEING HEARD

I BURIED HER IN A FRENCH PRESS

A MEMOIR ABOUT FINDING MY VOICE AND THE POWER OF BEING HEARD

SARAH BARNES-HUMPHREY

COPYRIGHT © 2025 SARAH BARNES-HUMPHREY
All rights reserved.

I BURIED HER IN A FRENCH PRESS
A Memoir About Finding My Voice and the Power of Being Heard

FIRST EDITION

ISBN 978-1-5445-4947-7 *Hardcover*
   978-1-5445-4946-0 *Paperback*
   978-1-5445-4948-4 *Ebook*
   978-1-5445-4949-1 *Audiobook*

For those who lifted me and those who tested me. Every moment shaped these pages.

To the lessons, both bitter and bold—thank you.

And to my husband. Your love has been the quiet strength behind every word. This is for you.

CONTENTS

Author's Note 11
Introduction 13

1. You Can Carry Strength and Struggle at the Same Time 25
2. You Can Feel Broken One Day and Brave the Next 39
3. Shine Without Apology 55
4. Everyone Doubts; Not Everyone Quits 67
5. Boxes Are for Shipping, Not for Living 77
6. Life Is Lived Forward and Understood Backwards 83
7. Boundaries Aren't Walls but Blueprints 97
8. Progress over Perfection 107
9. I Buried Her in a French Press 117
10. Labels Don't Define Your Identity; You Do 127
11. You Can Choose Grace over Grit 133

This Isn't the End; It's Just the Beginning 143
Acknowledgments 149
About the Author 151

AUTHOR'S NOTE

THIS BOOK IS A COLLECTION OF TRUTHS AS I REMEMBER them, filtered through time, perspective, and a generous splash of emotion. Names and some details have been changed to protect the privacy of those involved. (Whether they'd thank me or not is another story.)

These pages reflect my lived experiences, stitched together with memory and meaning. It's not a perfect record but an honest one.

If you see yourself in these stories, take it as a reminder of the impact we have on one another—for better, for growth, for good.

INTRODUCTION

NO ONE WAS MORE SURPRISED THAN I WAS THAT I DISCOVered the answer to my biggest health mystery in an episode of *Love Island UK*. For fifteen years I had been trying to figure out what was wrong with my legs. They first started changing in high school. People told me I had big thighs (highschoolers are cruel), but I never thought much of it since I was the catcher on my softball team. I squatted 150 times a game—that'll give anyone big quads and glutes. As for the sudden onset of excessive cellulite, I figured it was genetics and that all of this was just my lot in life.

But then in my mid-twenties, my ankles began to thicken. I started to see what I can only describe as shelves developing, as if fat were sinking down my legs and collecting there. My doctor didn't know what was happening, so she sent me to a variety of specialists. I saw a vein doctor who told me to run more because runners don't have fat legs. I was very fit and already playing sports five nights a week. Not helpful. A cardiologist told me if I simply stopped putting food in my mouth, I'd lose ten pounds and be a happy girl. But I was super skinny from my head to my hips. Unhelpful *and* rude. Then a neurologist said that if I ever got pregnant, I'd have treestump legs for the rest of my life. Unhelpful, rude, and terrifying.

I saw Shaolin doctors for acupuncture. I received regular lymphatic drainage massages. Nothing helped. I saw a kidney specialist who ordered an MRI to determine if there was water inside my legs. After seeing the image, he asked if he could show it to his students because, underneath all the mystery flesh, I actually have textbook-perfect thighs. Unhelpful but at least flattering.

After one of my doctor appointments, I remember sitting alone in my car and just yelling. *Why can't anyone figure out what's happening to me?* Worse, it felt like no one was listening. The frustration affected my mental health, which was already taking a beating: I never wore shorts and was embarrassed in any skirt or dress that revealed my cellulite or "cankles." I once wore a mid-calf dress to a conference, and when I returned to my hotel room at the end of the night, I saw that because I'd been on my feet all day, my lower legs were huge, swollen, sore, and, I thought, ugly. I felt incredible shame and embarrassment, assuming that everyone at the conference had been like, *Who is this girl with the cankles?* I cried all the time.

WHATEVER WE HIDE, WE FAIL TO UNDERSTAND, MUCH LESS VALUE.

We cover the parts of ourselves we dislike. So I hid my legs under clothes. And I pretended nothing was happening by not talking about it. That's partly why I stopped seeing specialists. I was tired of explaining it and being examined. But whatever we hide, we fail to understand, much less value.

By the time I was thirty-six, I had basically given up. I didn't want to see another doctor because I couldn't face more disappointment. I couldn't hear another specialist blame me for the problem instead of admitting they didn't know what was wrong. I really struggled with the blame. I kept being told the problem was me. At first, I believed it. But in the back of my mind, I knew the weight wasn't a result of a poor diet or not working out—it wasn't my choice. Still, at a certain point, I simply decided, *I can't solve this problem. I will have to learn to love the parts of me I don't like.* How in the heck I would actually do that, I didn't know.

Then a friend recommended a naturopath who works with UFC fighters, and I agreed to try *one more* specialist. He ordered a saliva cortisol test and a food sensitivity panel and discovered that my cortisol had been in the dumps for years and also that I was sensitive to several different foods. We started fixing all of that, and I lost eight centimeters on my calves alone. The shelves didn't entirely go away, but I learned about autoimmune issues and the role of inflammation in the body. At least it was a clue.

Not long after, in 2021, I was visiting family in England and watching *Love Island UK* with my cousin Lucy. She told me about a contestant the previous year, Shaughna Phillips, whose legs looked exactly like mine. On the show, she had discussed a rare illness. I checked out her Instagram profile, saw a few pictures, and instantly knew she and I suffered from the same condition. From there, I went to her YouTube and watched videos about something called lipedema and the surgery she underwent to address it. I started doing my own research and learned that it's an autoimmune disease, cause unknown. It keeps fat from returning to the bloodstream. And so it leads to a pathological increase in fatty tissue on the legs and, in some cases, arms, which is associated with severe pain for those affected. Four months later I had my first surgery.

Very little was known about lipedema at the time—in spite of the fact that, as we now know, 11 percent of women suffer from it. (The lack of knowledge results in part from the fact that women's bodies simply haven't been studied as much as men's have.) And the illness is still taboo. For example, I see it on women all the time, and I want to share information and resources with them, but what am I going to say? I can't approach someone with, "Hey, I think you have lipedema because your legs look fat." The best you can do is talk about it yourself—put yourself out there—and hope that others will recognize themselves in your story.

Fortunately, awareness is building. For example, right before this book went to press, Germany released some good news: soon lipedema patients with national health insurance will be able to undergo surgical treatment—with liposuction—under certain conditions, regardless of the stage of their chronic disease. Currently, liposuction is only covered by health insurance for stage three lipedema and as a temporary exception.

By the time I got my own diagnosis, I was in stage two of the condition's development, when extreme inflammation occurs up and down the legs and scar tissue begins forming. I flew to Beverly Hills for the first of two planned surgeries for water-assisted liposuction, which is one of the only ways to remove scar tissue and allow fat to move more smoothly and routinely through the body.

My best friend, Audrey, came out to stay with me. We rented an Airbnb. I was really nervous going into it. They don't put you out completely but into a twilight state so you know what's happening and can move around. Afterward, they stuffed me into a compression suit, which was difficult and very painful. It went from my feet all the way to my boobs and then all along my arms. Getting it on and off twice a day—to change the bandages on little incisions all over my body—was excruciating. I couldn't fly home for five days. I stayed on the pullout couch because it was the easiest place to stay put and watch TV or work; there wasn't much else I could do. We covered it in padding to absorb fluid that continued to leak out, post-surgery.

By the fourth day, I was able to walk around the neighborhood a bit. At the airport, I experienced what it's like for someone to travel in a wheelchair: how you're treated, how you need to advocate for yourself every step of the way, how much longer it takes, how vulnerable you are at the mercy of the airport staff. I had engaged in several conversations about disability on my *Blended* podcast—this is where I bring five people together from different walks of life to talk about inclusion in the workplace—but the experience gave me a new firsthand appreciation. Later, on the plane, after takeoff, I had a panic attack. I turned to Audrey and said, "I can't sit on the plane for five hours. I'm going to get a blood clot and die."

She said, "You're on blood thinners. If anybody is going to die from a blood clot, it'll be me." Laughing and crying while holding her hand helped calm me down. I did all three throughout the whole flight.

When I got home, I had to change the bandages and compression suit. My husband, Allan, helped. It was the first time he had seen me like that. It took us about an hour to do it all, in part because I had to take frequent breaks to lay on the ground and cry through the pain. I couldn't walk properly for almost six weeks. I just focused on trying to get through the twice weekly lymphatic-drainage massages, the removal and application of compression suits, and the frequent panic attacks I was now having at work and in the middle of live shows. At one point, I thought I'd never get full feeling back in my legs. But by May, I was playing softball again. And in September, I returned to Los Angeles for the second surgery. Then, in November, on my forty-second birthday, I wore a black knee-length dress. It was longsleeved, low-cut, and formfitting. I paired it with heels. I looked killer. I even posted it on Instagram. I finally had my confidence back—and my ankles too.

But the journey isn't over. Turns out I'm part of the one percent who have to return even after two surgeries. I'm currently waiting to schedule my third, which the surgeon can't perform until my inflammation decreases. I'm battling the inflammation by managing my cortisol through supplements, paying attention to my food sensitivities, working with a personal trainer, and receiving regular infrared sauna treatments. Regardless, I have different feelings now toward my condition.

Before, while the surgeries were happening, I didn't talk much about any of it. I didn't feel confident enough to. I finally shared my journey with lipedema in January 2023, in one of my *Monthly P.O.P.* LinkedIn newsletters. I've learned to accept it and value that part of myself as part of my journey. Even so, I can become completely obsessed with trying to fix it. It's a push and pull.

I try to accept the things I can't change and love myself as I am while also trying to solve the problem—not only for myself but for others suffering from lipedema. I think you need both acceptance and obsession when facing ongoing struggle. Both are needed to develop the kind of resilience that will keep you from drowning and giving up, that will allow you to keep moving forward. And we also need to have grace for ourselves—there are certainly days when I feel like covering up my legs completely.

This advice is for everyone, but I feel like it's especially important for women to hear it. Men have an easier time letting things go. And I don't think it's their default mode to self-blame. For years, I blamed myself for my condition. (Hell, I blamed myself for everything—we will definitely get into that later.) Even after I got to the point where I realized it wasn't a result of my life choices, I still blamed myself—surely there was something I wasn't doing, trying, or thinking about.

We all face adversity. Sometimes you won't conquer it. It'll just be part of your life. But you still keep fighting.

ACCEPTANCE AND STRUGGLE CAN GO HAND IN HAND.

Acceptance and struggle can go hand in hand. Even when you can't win, that doesn't have to define you. Even if some days it *does* define you, that's OK too.

We can't ever have all the answers. Sometimes there *isn't* a right answer. Part of the experience of being human is not to have all the answers.

* * *

This book is about self-worth and, more specifically, building a path toward it, a path that you continuously walk. In these pages, I have collected stories from my life that represent my own journey on this path. These stories are not about the other people in them or about others' relationships with me; I've included stories because of how I responded or reacted.

For that matter, sometimes I won't expand on a story because I don't feel it's mine to tell. I struggled while deciding what to include in this book and worried what certain people would think. I fretted over how to honor my story without crossing the line into what *wasn't* my story, without hurting someone else. Sometimes, when we tell stories involving other people, we mistakenly make them our own—and we tie them to our self-worth. But half of that story is somebody else's. The only thing I can control is how I react and my relationship with myself. And that is itself part of the journey toward self-worth because getting caught up in somebody else's reaction—and worrying about outside validation—can distract you from your path.

This journey is built with stepping stones. Sometimes I even took several steps back before having to restart. I truly believe life is a journey, not a destination. Nobody is perfect. And I'm *really* not perfect. I hope you'll be able to laugh at me a bit while reading these stories—because, when we're laughing, we realize that the journey toward self-worth doesn't have to be so heavy and serious.

Self-knowledge is power. But knowing yourself is only half the battle because sometimes, after you have developed enough to know who you are, you start asking if you actually *love* who you are. We sometimes have struggles in life and blame ourselves. We feel ashamed. We internalize it. Often, this keeps us from knowing what we truly want out of life.

And we can't help but compare ourselves to others without realizing that comparison is the thief of self-worth. I used to spend so much time scrolling Instagram, and by the time I closed the app, I almost always felt worse. Jealous. Frustrated. In my head. It didn't make me feel more connected or inspired. It made me feel small and stuck. The worst part was that I knew it. I knew I wasn't feeling good, and yet I kept going back. That kind of pull is hard to break. But once I realized just how much control I had handed over to an app, it clicked for me. I didn't need to keep doing that to myself.

But that doesn't mean I didn't get knocked down in other ways. Of course I did—it's inevitable. Sometimes, we don't actually know how to get back up. We tend to ask, "Why is it always me? Why am I the common denominator? Why don't I get the things I want out of life?" Questions like that are natural responses.

But ultimately they only keep us from learning lessons after getting knocked down. And if we can't do that, then we also can't use those lessons to impact and empower ourselves, which leads to empowering other people. Yes, there will be days when you want to stay in bed. There will also be days when you're confident. It's OK for your self-worth to rise and fall. The struggle will be much harder if self-worth is something you feel pressured to nail every day. *It's not.*

Still, the challenge to feel worthy can be overwhelming. This is true even after achieving quote-unquote success because even then we still lose confidence sometimes. We still feel like we don't belong in whatever room we are in. Getting pulled in different directions at work can cause us to second-guess ourselves. Although we're trusted to be the one making decisions, we doubt our choices. We tend to take on too much and say yes to everything but then can't do it all and end up letting people down. Meanwhile, we procrastinate doing the things we really want to.

Worse, when we experience setbacks, we start to think *we* are the problem. But setbacks are inevitable. Still, if they occur at a time when we struggle with self-worth, it becomes even more challenging to think outside of the box and bounce back.

I want this book to help you feel seen and therefore understand that you're not alone, that almost everyone goes through these internal struggles. My hope is that you walk away knowing how to think about things differently in order to move forward. My wish is that this book will help you figure out how to bounce back—not once and for all but again and again. Achieving self-worth is not a box that can be checked off a to-do list. I want to support you through your journey.

ALL YOU NEED TO DO IN ANY MOMENT IS SHOW UP.

You will come to understand that it's OK if you don't love yourself some days. You can bounce back and dive into your self-worth the next day. All you need to do in any moment is show up—whether that's for yourself or for someone else. Show up even when you don't want to because the next opportunity might be around the corner, but you won't meet it if you take too much time to wallow on the couch.

Instead of getting caught up in the negative feelings surrounding struggle, we can focus on learning from them. We can change the way we understand adversity and challenges, see how they actually make us better people, and empower us to understand ourselves better so we can not only help ourselves but also impact other people. Doing so minimizes our instincts to degrade ourselves and our self-worth, and instead it empowers us to get through unhappy days (which are natural) and keep moving forward on our journeys.

The book is about one woman's path toward self-worth. I am still on it. We all are. I hope that you'll feel more convinced you don't have to do this alone. After reading this book, I hope you will feel differently about challenges and then take actions toward them. No one has reached the destination of self-worth. All we can do is keep moving forward.

* * *

Sometimes we need to hear things from other people. Case in point, I didn't know I had a superpower or understand its connection to my adversity until I heard someone else say it. And, OK, I'll admit it: this person was an energy healer. It was 2024. Someone told me I *had* to go see this woman, and that was that. I made an appointment.

The healer told me that because my personal and professional lives have been so messy, I'm now able to create safe spaces for others. That hit me hard. I realized, *The universe is telling me that the trauma I've experienced is part of my path in life—and not my fault.* Even when I was treated badly by certain people along the way and couldn't understand why, all of it had a purpose.

Then, I thought more about this bit of wisdom in September, while I was attending the Summit of Greatness, a self-development conference led by Lewis Howes. (I'm a big fan. He is the reason I got into podcasting. I love his podcast *The School of Greatness*. One day, I thought, *If Lewis Howes can have his own podcast, so can I*.) That weekend, I saw that one of the biggest effects of my podcasts and panel moderating has been the creation of safe spaces for my guests and panel members. This is especially true in the work I've done to bring marginalized voices to the microphone.

That weekend, I came to understand that my ability, desire,

and motivation to create safe spaces is a direct result of the empathy I gained from my own personal and professional struggles. Understanding that people need to feel seen and heard, which I realized only after recognizing the same desire in myself, I developed the ability to empower them or create space for them to do that. Now, I understand this as my superpower.

I believe we all have superpowers. We weren't born with them. Rather, they developed because of the adversities we've faced. I quickly decided I wanted to use this power on a larger scale. I wanted to write a book. I thought about how much listeners of my *Women in Supply Chain* podcast have been helped by the conversations I've had with guests about their journeys and trials. I thought about all the touching comments I've received from readers of my *Monthly P.O.P.* newsletter, who shared that my personal stories of struggle resonated with them. And I especially thought about my *Blended* podcast, which is nothing short of magical to me.

In each episode, the five guests have never met each other, most have never met me, and we talk about really difficult topics for two hours. The guests themselves tell me these conversations about inclusion have changed their lives. We tackle hard topics, such as privilege. After I hit the stop-recording button, guests turn to me and say, "I really felt seen and heard today." After hearing that again and again, following every episode, I came to truly understand the impacts. Just as a result of participating and hearing from others, my guests change the conversations they have internally and with their teams. So I decided to scale up even more to reach more people. You, dear reader, are one of them.

**YOUR STRUGGLES ARE A PATH
TO YOUR SUPERPOWERS.**

Although I write a lot about setbacks, I don't perceive them as inherently negative. Rather, they are opportunities. (Admittedly, if you try to tell me that in the moment, I'll see red. But once I have had a chance to digest a situation and work on myself, then can I see them as opportunities.) We can take setbacks on our paths and use them to discover our superpowers. I'm using my superpower in these pages. And I hope that reading them will also create a safe space for you.

I want you to see your struggles as a path to your own superpowers. Your journey to self-worth can lay pebbles in front of you. And they will be noticed if you take the time to notice them. Sometimes they will give you reassurance, and sometimes they will let you know what isn't right for you—as long as you are listening. I hope you will rethink your relationship with adversity and begin using it to figure all of this out. Fortunately, there's no rush because the path never ends. I'll say it again: the journey to self-worth has no destination.

I certainly haven't reached the end of my journey with lipedema. First of all, the problem isn't solved. Even if I get that third surgery, I probably won't be cured. So my relationship between lipedema and my self-worth is continuously evolving. I continue to meet the struggle head-on and work toward solutions while also trying to accept and love myself as I am. When I succeed at that, I feel confident that I can do anything put in front of me. When I fail at it, it can be enough just to get out of bed that day. And that's OK. I've at least learned along the way that I can take a step backward and still be on my path.

CHAPTER 1

YOU CAN CARRY STRENGTH AND STRUGGLE AT THE SAME TIME

IT WAS THE WORST DAY OF MY LIFE. EVERYBODY WAS PACKing up their desks and leaving, and I was just crying. I couldn't help myself. One of the VPs was going around telling everyone that I needed to get a therapist because I was crying too much. There were a lot of emotions that day. There was shame in the fact that we couldn't keep the business going. Even though it was the family business, I felt like people blamed me personally because I was the oldest and had been there the longest. That means I also thought I was partly responsible for it.

And many of these people were like family to me because I'd been there for more than twenty years. I had basically grown up there. And then right after high school, I went straight into the family business. I didn't go to college; I went to the reception desk at my family's company. Suddenly, I was losing everything I had worked toward and everything I'd hoped for. Since I was sixteen, I had wanted to take over the company. I had never even been in a job interview before. I'd developed other side hustles over the years, but they were mostly further education for what I ultimately wanted for my future: to take over the company.

Then everything fell apart. The details of the downfall aren't pertinent here. It's not my story to tell, and, anyway, it would all probably bore you. Short story, outside forces decided the business had grown too risky and left it hanging unsupported, forcing it to close.

We had been a logistics company, a travel agent for cargo or products. After working the reception desk, I spent eight years in operations, where I moved products by truck, then ocean, and then air. Then I transitioned into sales for eight years. During the last few, I had more of a leadership role. And I was tasked with the further development of our brand identity. To the C suite, marketing was considered a cost center. (For example, some of the senior leadership asked if we even needed a website. This was 2015/2016. So you can imagine the uphill battle I was waging.)

My team was small but mighty. One day I saw a podcast kit on Amazon and decided we were going to start our own podcast. Marketing in supply chain and logistics at the time was stuffy. I thought this was our chance to make a mark.

I'd been listening to a lot of podcasts (like Lewis Howes's *School of Greatness*). It was really the perfect way to tell our brand's story. I asked a guy from the customs department to be my cohost. The phrase *supply chain* references the entire thread of sourcing, buying, moving, housing, and delivering a product. (Think of the cup you are drinking from as you read or listen to this book—it came to you through a supply chain. In fact, I've probably influenced some part of its path.) So the team and I decided to call the podcast, in a tongue-in-cheek way, *2 Babes Talk Supply Chain*—I wanted to see how far we could push the industry. Like I said, back in 2016, industry marketing was pretty stuffy.

Our first two episodes—and I think you can still find them on

YouTube—were awful, terrible quality. We used Skype because I thought it was the only option; we sat in front of the computer while the guest was on the screen. But we kept going. I kept inviting guests. And then, because my boss had just built a studio for his son in their house, we ended up recording in the studio with live guests. We actually had a professional production. After the business shut its doors in late 2017, guests started to pay $100 each to come on the show.

It came as a shock to most in the company. We had 150 employees across Canada. Without warning, it disappeared. I'm not going to get into the nitty-gritty because, first of all, I don't know it all, but mostly, it's not my story to tell. I can say this much, at least: I was gutted. My dream was over. My stability was gone. My reality shifted entirely and immediately.

I struggled—with the weight of not having anywhere to be on a daily basis, with not knowing who I was outside of the company. On top of all of that, I was then smacked down in a completely different industry. About a year earlier, everyone at my family's company was switched to a four-day work week. Since my husband, Allan, and I both worked there, our income took a 20 percent cut. So I looked for a secondary flexible source of income. A friend recommended I become a life insurance agent. That area not only interested me but is one in which I knew I could help people. So I studied for and earned my license, and I started to lay the groundwork in that industry.

When my family's company closed its doors, I thought, *Thank goodness, I have a backup plan.* I threw myself into that work, as well as a few other side hustles (more on those later). Staying busy helped me so much during those first few months after the layoffs. But then, later in the year, my new insurance work landed me in crosshairs. I was targeted and sued on bogus claims. It stalled my insurance dream and to this day has not been resolved. (Hopefully I'll be able to discuss it all in my next book.)

Somewhere in all of the emotion and drama, I wondered, *What do I do about the podcast?* I felt responsible to all of the guests we'd already booked. Even though I had lost my cohost and my team, I wanted to keep the podcast going. Suddenly, it was a one-person show. I had to learn graphic design, social media, website design, you name it. I had lost everybody who had been doing those things. And then I had to find an editor pretty quickly because that was the one task I refused to do.

As for the other skills, I just started *doing* them. I read a few articles about Canva to help me with graphics. I got on Wix and figured out how to create a website. Whenever I hit a wall or got to some part I didn't understand, I would turn to Google or YouTube. And, look, to be clear, nobody, even today, would hire me for graphic design, social-media work, or website design. But I did learn enough to get by and keep moving forward.

In January 2018, I launched a series *within* the podcast titled *Women in Supply Chain*. I wanted to hear more about women's career journeys in our industry. I thought that was important because I wanted women in the industry to understand what was possible in their careers. Also, at the last few conferences I had attended, only a few other women were there, and I knew that needed to change.

So I was mostly just interested. I wanted to learn more about the kind of women in the industry, what they did for a living, how they got there, what their journeys looked like. I knew my own journey wasn't necessarily straight. And because I had worked for the family business my whole career, I hadn't really been exposed to many other people in the rest of the supply chain. I figured if I wanted to learn from them, then some of my listeners would too. I launched the series. But I only had a few guests before the well ran dry—because either women didn't want to come on a show called *2 Babes Talk Supply Chain* or their employers wouldn't let them.

So I rebranded and changed the podcast name to *Let's Talk Supply Chain*. I did it in a week, which was the craziest week of my life because all sorts of other changes were required. I was putting everything into the podcast. I was all in because I was passionate about it, but also because I wasn't sure the insurance path would work out—and I couldn't find a traditional job. I'd been applying all over the place. Nobody was calling me back.

Remember that I had never even applied for a job before that year. I had only been in one interview in my life. And now I was thirty-seven years old. Fortunately, I had some money put away, and had my husband Allan's steady income to fall back on...for a while, at least. He left my family's business before it fell apart and had already found new work. But then he lost that job right before the pandemic. All in all, it was a challenging time.

I applied for a part-time job at Canada Post, the post office inside the local drug store called Shopper's Drug Mart. Shopper's Drug Mart did at least call me in but said I wasn't what they were looking for. I learned, three months later, that the lady in charge hadn't hired me because she thought I would eventually take her job.

It was now August 2018. I had been out of a job for ten months. I had days where I was completely stuck in fear, wondering *What am I going to do if I can't get a job?* Those days were the hardest. They were paralyzing—I would go to bed at night without having done anything since I'd woken up. That was very foreign to me. I'm a doer. But that's the power of fear. I know how hard it is to be out of work and looking for a job. I know the hit your confidence and self-worth take and the spiral you can slip into as a result.

Finally, I applied to be a receptionist at the local indoor tennis club. I was hired on the spot. It felt so good to have anyone interested in me and my skills, even if the work was rudimentary. I answered phones, took people's payments. Once they erected the tennis bubble, it was my job to check it every now and then, maintain the pressure inside it, or call someone to fix it. When it snowed, I shoveled and salted the walkways between the clubhouse and the bubble.

And I had to shovel out all of the doors on the bubble, the fire exits. There were other duties. On the one hand, I got CPR training, which was cool. On the other hand, I maintained the bathrooms and mopped the floors—less cool. But, hey, I was happy for the gig. I made $15 an hour and worked three or four days a week.

Then I picked up another job scoring men's basketball. That's the most terrifying thing I've ever done. Because these players thought they were going to the NBA. They were deathly serious and would get mad at me for every little thing. I had to press the buzzer at exactly the right time, put in the score in exactly a certain way. I definitely made a few mistakes—and these men were scary when they were mad! Fortunately, the refs were nice and would tell them to eff off if they were being jerks.

But as harrowing as it was—and as humbling to go from being a corporate director to mopping floors—I was thankful. Especially because the paycheck allowed me to keep building the podcast, which became my business. At the time, I didn't know where it was going or what it would do. Still, I worked on it every single day. At the reception desk, when I wasn't busy, I was sending out emails or working on scripts or graphics. I even had my laptop with me while I scored basketball. (Come to think of it, maybe that's why they yelled at me. Just kidding, I paid attention when I needed to. Mostly.)

Even if I was happy to have work and the ability to pursue a creative project meanwhile, the part-time jobs were tough on my ego. People talked down to me at reception. I remember one night, mopping the floors, thinking *If my former colleagues could see me now*.

But throughout, the podcast grew. By June 2019, I had 1,200 followers on LinkedIn and probably 3,500 listeners. Eventually, I tested out the live environment on LinkedIn. And every Monday I released an episode of the podcast. I told myself that all I had to do was keep releasing episodes on Mondays. Fortunately, whenever I faltered, I'd get some nugget of encouragement: someone reaching out to say how much they loved an episode or to say they wanted to be a sponsor on the show.

Plus, I was learning so much from the guests. I genuinely enjoyed it. I thought, *Well if I can have fun with this, and it can take me in a direction I've always wanted to go, from an entrepreneurial standpoint, then I'll keep it going.* And if I could keep increasing my rates and eventually hire people to help me, then why not? I saw that it could be a business—or, at least, I was starting to.

But by that point I was already traveling and being paid to speak at conferences. Then the pandemic shut everything down. I was in Long Beach, California, for TPM (formerly the Trans-Pacific Maritime conference) that happens every March, when they started talking about the shutdowns. I decided to head to San Diego before Long Beach—and found out the day before I had to be at the conference that it was canceled. I still ended up traveling to Long Beach, and in fact, quite a few people had also landed already. So we all hung out and then participated in a virtual conference that a friend had put together at the last minute so we could all make good on the hard work that had gone into planning that conference. It was an example of exactly the kind of community that helped me build the career I have today and that I try to support as much as possible.

I didn't have another speaking gig until January 2021 at Manifest. After arriving, we all had to get COVID-19 tests before we were allowed to register. Some who tested positive flew all the way to Vegas for nothing, since they had to quarantine. During the pandemic, everything really started happening for me. Most brands in supply chain were moving towards digital content, and I happened to be perfectly positioned to help them with that. I could build the business remotely. That's when *Let's Talk Supply Chain* took off.

Of course, the lockdown also shuttered my "day" jobs: both the tennis club and the basketball games. I was scared, but I had some other side hustles going. I figured at least one of them had to take off. I just needed to keep all of the plates in the air until that happened. *Let's Talk Supply Chain* was the one that took off.

It didn't happen overnight. I struggled so hard to figure out what the heck I was doing. I used to write out all of the scripts by hand and then type them into an email to the guest. It was super inefficient. I wondered if promotional videos would help, so I started recording myself teasing the next episode. I was very uncomfortable on camera, which certainly came through in those first videos. I was testing out equipment. I was testing out episodes. I had horrible lighting. And I was doing it all at my kitchen table—with a view of stairs behind me.

I was just trying to figure out how to make money by podcasting and creating content. At the time, though, I don't think I even knew I was creating content. *Supply-chain media* wasn't even a term yet. But I just kept getting up every day and doing one more thing. Usually that was making a phone call: to ask someone what I could do for them or what they were looking for in marketing or if they would come on the podcast. At first, I didn't know what people in the industry were looking to get out of a podcast episode.

Eventually, I realized that supply-chain professionals wanted to learn about other companies, who else was in the market, and who they wanted to work with. That was the evolution, and it stemmed from my own curiosity. When I asked guests about their companies, I got great responses from listeners and discovered that that curiosity was not only mine but also the market's. I also realized that those conversations were why guests would pay to come on.

I didn't share strong opinions about these companies or recommend to guests that they work or not work with anyone in particular. I still don't. I just create the platform for people to tell their stories, allowing others to hear them and decide for themselves what they want to do with that information. It's not about me. I didn't create *Let's Talk Supply Chain* because I wanted to be the face of something. I became the face because I was the only one who would work for free for those first three years. My goal was always to create a platform that elevates voices in the industry in an authentic way. I'm just a conduit to that.

People liked what I was doing. Slowly, I built a brand. I had this big teal boom arm that came in the podcast kit I'd ordered off of Amazon. It was ugly and cumbersome. But it was front and center every week. Eventually, I became known for having that type of microphone. I've upgraded now (and changed to black from teal blue), but my mic is still the same look and style.

It was the end of one chapter—working for my family business—and the beginning of a new chapter. I had no idea where it would take me. I had no idea that this thing I had built from nothing would go on to win awards and make me an industry leader. I had no idea that this little podcast would lead me to break glass ceilings in the space because nobody had done it before. And I could not have predicted the incredible joy and fulfillment I would get from building a platform for the voices of others, especially those marginalized in our industry.

From the outside, it might have looked like I believed in myself throughout, but sometimes I have no idea how I got through. *It was hard.* When my family's company closed, I was out on my ass with no team, no cohost, and no paycheck. Suddenly, I had to learn graphic design, website design, social media, you name it. The positive messages I received from listeners helped a lot. I heard from women in the supply-chain industry who told me how much they resonated with the series. Sometimes it was just that they were new to supply chain and needed to learn about the industry itself. Either way, knowing I had helped them kept my spirits up.

And of course, the *Women in Supply Chain* series is only one of several. I was hearing from all sorts of listeners who were learning—and enjoying learning—about different companies, thought leadership, and trending news in our industry. People related to the energy I brought. They liked how I explained things. Mostly, they liked the conversations. This was the reassurance I needed to know I was on the right path. I used to be wired to think I needed to feel confident in something before I tried it. Now I just try things and let the confidence catch up.

It felt like nuggets were being placed in front of me. Some telling me to stay on certain paths. Some telling me to get off other paths. I had to start paying attention to the nuggets and figure out how to identify them. I guess that's why responses from readers meant so much. When somebody takes time out of their day to reinforce what you're doing, that's a nugget for sure. Don't discount that.

I developed a habit that has since become a philosophy: respond personally to every comment and message. If someone takes time out of their day to make a comment or send a message, then I can definitely take time out of mine to respond. Of course, the dialogue has to be constructive, but it almost always is. Nowadays, even though I have a team—and some of them specifically help me with social media content—I still respond personally to as many comments as I can. It's a sign of respect. And I think it's how I have built trust. I also pressure the team to ensure all comments receive a response from someone. And I make sure they understand why it's important.

But know that nuggets like that don't always have to come over LinkedIn. If you have a dog-walking business and the owner gives you a compliment or the dog is really excited to see you, that's information. That's confirmation.

When I worked for the family business, I was always kind of in my parents' shadow. It was always their show. Everything we did was to build their dream. A family business can be a difficult environment. A lot of people look at you and think you're so lucky, that you get everything. And there is some truth to that. But also you're being judged on a daily basis, and you don't know whom you can trust because everybody wants something from you. I once had a supervisor say she was jealous of the fact that my parents owned the company, and I thought, *Well, that's a lot of bias—I guess I can't report to you anymore.*

On a daily basis, I had to do two or three times more than everybody else, just to prove myself worthy of the position. To be fair, though, a lot of that stemmed from me not believing in myself and thinking that everybody else's opinion of me mattered. Then suddenly I was out on my own. I had to learn to trust myself. It took a long time.

But I didn't spend that time sitting around doing nothing. I am the type of person who, if I tell somebody I'm going to do something, I do it, no matter how I'm feeling at any given moment. I had people paying to come on the show! Granted, it was only $100 each. Still, my conviction to follow through for them kept me going, kept me out of bed. That's always been a strong value of mine: to do what I say I'm going to do. Even in times of my life when I don't have all the self-worth in the world, I still have that core value to adhere to.

Society often tells us we need to have "purpose." And that if you don't, you're not worthy, and what the hell are you doing with your life? But I think you can have a few different purposes, and also they're constantly changing. I tend to think about the idea of purpose as something that's co-related to core values. I don't know what my quote-unquote purpose is, but I know my core values, and if I keep following those, I won't get lost. And my core values will lead me toward the impact I want to make in the world. First, they led me to a business that allowed me to make money, which ultimately led to my advocacy work.

YOUR CORE VALUES WILL LEAD YOU TO YOUR PURPOSE.

Try not to get caught up or stressed out by trying to figure out what your purpose is. I think sometimes we fight too hard to find it instead of letting it happen naturally, figuring out over time what resonates the most. Following your core values will lead you to it and also keep you on the path to self-worth.

And so, even though those first podcast episodes were *really* bad, my core values pushed me to keep putting them out. And slowly, I started believing in myself. A little bit every day. It doesn't happen overnight. And even once you have it, it can go away. One day, my relationship with self-worth will feel at 100 percent, and the next day it'll be 45 percent...and 85 the day after that.

Think about something you feel confident in, something you do without thinking because you just know you're good at it. Whatever it is, you weren't always good at it. There was a journey to get there. You didn't start off knowing how to do anything. That's kind of what the journey to self-worth is like.

BELIEVING IN YOURSELF COMES FROM ACCEPTING THAT LOSS DOESN'T DEFINE YOU.

And yes, sometimes you'll falter even at the things you're really good at. For example, even though I'm a really good softball catcher and have been playing for thirty-plus years, I can always have a bad game. I'm confident in the skill and have worked at it for a very long time, but I can still miss a ball, and then the team loses. Believing in yourself doesn't necessarily come after the win. It comes from accepting that, when you have a loss, that loss doesn't define you. You still have the skill. Even Simone Biles got the "twisties."

Whatever the skill, whether it's self-worth or something more tangible, once it develops, it's contagious. That's what happened with the podcast. I learned website design and got a little confidence from that. Then I felt self-assured enough to tackle social-media promotion. I slowly picked up skills. No matter the task, you'll almost always have to figure it out as you go.

Hold progress over perfection. Even when you're uncomfortable, move forward anyway. It doesn't have to be perfect. People will either see value in it or they won't. They don't need it to be perfect to make that valuation. Even when the graphics were bad, I put out the podcast. Even when the audio was horrible, I put out the podcast. I took feedback and built upon my skills every week.

Anyway, since I was one of the first people to have a podcast in supply chain, *everything* I did was progress over perfection because I didn't have anyone to emulate. I also didn't have a choice. To keep the schedule, I had to keep putting it out. And I didn't have money to pay anybody to actually do it well. Each week before I published, I would think, *It's not gold standard, but I tried my best.*

If I'd put too much emphasis on being perfect, it would've been too much pressure. I wouldn't be five hundred episodes in with fourteen team members. I would've quit. Perfection is paralyzing. We are always in continuous progress. In fact, don't even think about it as progress *toward* perfection. It's just *moving forward*. Learning, shifting, growing. Case in point: I am now also the first podcaster ever to franchise.

What is perfection anyway? It doesn't exist. Whatever definition you have of perfection in your head is probably only getting in your way. We spend too much time in a negative mindset of thinking we aren't good enough when really we should just be thinking about constant change. If we're making a bit more progress every day, we are succeeding. There is only progress. Every day, you're a different person.

As it's turned out over the years, the early episode with the worst audio is now our most listened to.

Certainly, those years were challenging. I went from being a director of sales and marketing, who traveled constantly and led a team of people, to having nothing. But I don't wish it hadn't happened. I've been able to make more of an impact through what I've done since. And I learned so much about myself along the way.

I've since been able to become the person I was all along but wasn't fully realizing because I was always in my parents' shadow and struggling to figure out who I really am. In some ways, it was an opportunity. When something like that happens, while you're doing whatever you have to do to keep the electricity on, remember that losing everything is sometimes your chance to build back up a life that's more fulfilling. You can find strength during struggle. Looking back, I know I did.

CHAPTER 2

YOU CAN FEEL BROKEN ONE DAY AND BRAVE THE NEXT

WHEN I WAS A KID, THERE WAS A WHOLE YEAR WHEN I barely talked. Halfway through sixth grade, my parents moved us from Ontario to Vancouver. I arrived full of anxiety. I had been bullied pretty badly at my previous elementary school (more on that later) and was afraid of what might happen at my new school. I did end up with a group of girls to hang out with in the schoolyard, but I barely spoke.

One on one, if I was over at their houses or whatever, I would talk. But in the group, I just followed them around. I felt so much pressure to fit in. And I had little confidence that anything I had to say was worth contributing. I figured, *If I don't speak or show people who I am, they won't have an opportunity to hate me.*

Slowly, those friends helped me get out of my shell. But the underlying impulse remained to keep things close to my chest. Anyway, the bullying eventually returned. I fell in with a group in high school, and one of them became my boyfriend. When he broke up with me, he turned the whole group against me. They took turns calling my house to ream me out. It was terrifying.

Halfway through eleventh grade, my parents moved back to Ontario to take over the business from a former partner. Collectively, we decided I would stay in Vancouver and live with my grandmother because if I moved to Ontario, I would've had to do an extra year of high school, and I would have had to make new friends and find community. It would have felt like starting over. In hindsight, I'm not sure it was the right decision. My parents and I all thought my grandmother was going to be there for me and do the traditional grandma things. But she didn't end up being that person. I didn't feel love for me in that house. It shocked us all.

And those years were hard on all of us anyway. I missed out on a few key years with my family, especially my brother. My parents were under a lot of pressure and were trying their best to make sure I was OK while going through a stressful situation three thousand miles away. And I had to give up on my dreams of going to the Olympics for softball.

The dream had been born a couple of years prior, when my mom signed me up to be a bat girl at the Canada Cup. I was gifted at the sport. (I still am. I've played competitive softball for thirty-five years and, at the age of forty-five, still throw guys out at second.) But I hadn't thought it could be a career. I hadn't considered walking out on an Olympic field—until that week at the Canada Cup.

It was the best week of my life. I was the bat girl for the Australian team, meaning I would literally go pick up the bats whenever they dropped them after running to first base. I was so nervous, which meant the whole thing was a big deal for me. And the team included me in warm-up, throwing the ball around with me. I felt like part of the team. It was incredible. When it was over and they left, I cried. It was the first time I'd ever felt like I was a part of something and in a place I was meant to be. They were great girls and played amazing softball, and I fit in.

Then my parents moved to a different city, and I lost my support network and advocates. The dream evaporated. In retrospect, I possibly could have figured out how to advocate for myself and reach out to recruits, how to be where I needed to be and be in front of whoever needed to see me. But at sixteen, I didn't know any of that. Instead, I just forgot about my dream.

Besides, there was so much else I was suddenly responsible for: cooking and cleaning for myself, getting myself to and from school, getting a job, getting a life. Long story short, I had to figure out that year and a half for myself. At sixteen, I had a lot of responsibility. And a lot of independence, probably too much.

I grew up quickly, learning to grocery shop and cook for myself, drive myself to and from softball games and anywhere I needed to be. This was happening at a time when I struggled to value myself and find myself as a person. I couldn't speak up for myself. I was terrified of confrontation. I was treated badly by people at school and didn't think I was valuable as a person at all. I considered suicide on a number of occasions. I used to sleep walk, so I started keeping a pair of scissors next to my bed, hoping that one night I would take the scissors and just do it. I often thought, *I don't deserve to be on the earth, and nobody wants me here.* I didn't understand *why* I was here.

And I didn't understand the hate I received from others or what I had done to deserve it. But at some point, it didn't matter why it happened because it just kept happening. Eventually, I fell into the wrong crowd. I think I was trying to escape how I actually felt about myself, and I didn't have a lot of support. I made some bad choices.

Softball helped get me through. It was the only thing I was good at. Everyone loved me on the field. And people listened to me. They *had* to because I was the catcher, lol. I called all the plays. It's funny, but in some ways, I found my voice literally: by screaming plays. Still, at times I felt they liked me only because I helped us win games, because I was good at what I did. I still understood my value as transactional.

NOT FEELING GOOD ABOUT OURSELVES CAN LEAD TO SELF-SABOTAGE.

One time during senior year, I tattled on the team. I can't remember exactly what happened, but I think they were smoking weed or something like that. They all turned on me. It was such a stupid choice. I feel like I did it subconsciously because I didn't think I deserved friends. I definitely got that outcome.

I have since come to believe that not feeling good about ourselves can lead to self-sabotage. Maybe we don't feel we deserve something, like a better job. So when we get the interview for the better job, we don't set ourselves up for success. As a result, we don't rise higher than wherever we subconsciously think we deserve to be.

For example, still to this day, I chew my cuticles and I bite my lips. These behaviors fit the classic definition of self-sabotage because they literally make me less physically attractive. And I specifically do them when I'm anxious.

We self-sabotage also when we feel imposter syndrome and when we feel we aren't good enough. There are so many subconscious reasons why. In the case of a job interview, maybe the person is scared of actually getting the job: how hard it would be, how out of place they would feel, that they might fail. If they ruin it for themselves, they won't have to face any of that. Or, of course, if they weren't going to get the job anyway, then self-sabotaging it at least helps them avoid the pain of rejection.

In my case, when I tattled on the team, I think, in retrospect, I was scared to actually have friends who cared about me. Being in real friendships is hard work. You have to be vulnerable with them. You have to open up and let them in. At the time, I was on my own. I didn't really have family around who cared about me. And I was accustomed to being bullied. Who was I to think I needed or deserved friends?

And before that, in tenth grade, I'd started dating a guy who ended up making me miserable. It's hard to even remember what I liked (or thought I liked) about him. He was arrogant and smarmy. But he was social and got along with different groups of people, which I guess I appreciated. And we had commonalities. His mom was single, so he had a lot of freedom too. We were both smoking too much weed. Honestly, I think he was using me to get weed, using me in a variety of ways. He liked that I had a car and always had cash.

But I didn't recognize any of that at the time. He made me feel valued…as much as it was possible at that time for me to feel valued. And of course, it was the wrong kind of value. The whole time, he was verbally abusive, gaslighting me and pretending to love me, saying whatever he needed to get me to do what he wanted. He put me down in front of other people and would laugh about it, saying I couldn't take a joke.

One day, during a fight, he threw his glasses at me. That was my first indication something was really wrong: it wasn't a punch, but still, he had escalated from verbal abuse to physical.

After graduation, we planned for him to move back to Ontario with me. I thought it was a great idea. But then, while I was gone for a couple of months, he started cheating on me immediately. That didn't help the ol' ego. I had suspicions that he'd done it throughout our relationship and during high school. The news and revelations were enough for me to finally walk away. I closed that chapter and, since I was moving back to Ontario, didn't have anything to do with anybody from that part of my life again.

I needed change. Naturally, the next thing I did was cut off all my hair. I got that *Kate Plus 8* haircut, the one made popular at the time by reality TV star Kate Gosselin. I don't know if I'd consider that evidence of a full-on spiral, but it was definitely my Britney Spears moment. I also started working as a receptionist at my parents' company. And then, inexplicably, I started going to raves—it rescued me. It completely turned around my life.

I had reconnected with a childhood neighbor friend of mine, who introduced me to this ska band. At one of their shows, we learned about raves. One night, we got invited to a big party. I thought it sounded fun and exciting and figured that if I drove myself there, what could it hurt, because I could leave anytime I wanted. I was living with my parents, and I'm pretty sure I didn't tell them where we were going that night. Not that they had much to worry about. I didn't do any of the drugs. I think I took a caffeine pill that night.

It was in a big industrial space. The music was incredible. Most people were high. I went with a couple of people I didn't know very well, and I found it all fascinating. It opened me up to a whole new world. My childhood friend and I only attended a few parties together because I was meeting so many new people and gravitating toward different groups. That first night, I didn't feel the need to go back to my car early. I stayed until the end. Before long, I was going every Friday and Saturday night for two years.

You won't be surprised to hear that I went to Michaels and bought a jar of sparkles that I applied to my eyelids. I changed the color of my short hair every other month or so, blonde to red to whatever. (Yes, it was horrendous.) And I felt true happiness and acceptance. I eventually ended up in all the VIP sections and knew all the promoters, producers, and DJs. I learned so much about the music. For example, I do not like Happy Hardcore. What, you don't know what Happy Hardcore is? I would tell you to look it up and listen so you'd understand, but I wouldn't wish that high-pitched stress-inducing sound on anyone.

All the other music I liked. Some parties were dedicated to one genre, and others explored several throughout the night. Raves were my happy place. The lights, the people. The music was so loud that you could feel it in your chest. Mostly, I loved all the people and the communal nature of it. And I quickly found out I love to dance. I would dance the night away.

I have always felt concerts are kind of an individual experience.

A rave to me felt like community, like everyone comes together around the music, dancing, and having a good time. There's no judgment. It was my first experience with a truly safe space. I learned so much about myself.

Sometimes I would go with people, sometimes meet people there. I'd show up with this little *Lion King* backpack I had that I kept full of lollipops. Then I'd walk around giving lollipops to everyone who wanted one. My friends who did drugs knew they could trust me, so they'd tell me whatever they had taken so I could inform the ambulance driver in case anything happened to them.

I felt taken care of by them in turn. I felt safe, liked, and free. By a certain point, I'd walk in a venue and know everyone inside. It felt amazing. None of these people wanted anything from me. They genuinely liked me for me. I didn't have to do drugs to fit in. Nobody cared. They certainly didn't care if I was the best dancer on the floor. Yes, the bathrooms were disgusting. And the floors at the end of the night—oh my God, so gross. But I was happy.

At the same time, I was working at my parents' company. They all knew I raved because I talked about it. I wasn't ashamed of it. It was my jam. It was my thing and I told everybody. What I didn't realize until later is that they were judging me. They all assumed I was doing drugs. Even after I told them I wasn't, one of the VPs kept making jokes during operations meetings that I hid ecstasy in my desk.

It was a weird time because I was being judged and devalued during the work week and then validated in my other community over the weekends. I worked so hard to prove myself during the day. I didn't realize at the time that if my coworkers didn't like me, they were never going to. Nothing I did could change that. I was no longer in high school, but I still had a target on my back. This time because I was the owners' daughter.

So I was living a bit of a double life. And then I met Paul. At a rave. I don't remember which one. We started going to different parties together. Then we started hanging out together outside of parties. Then we started dating. About a year or a year and a half later, my great aunt won the lottery in the UK with several other people. She gave all of her grandchildren $20,000. I put the money toward a down payment for a house, and Paul and I moved in together. I was only twenty-three years old when he proposed.

About three months before the wedding, my parents asked me to go to Vancouver and help pack up my grandmother's belongings because they were selling the house and moving her back to Ontario. Paul didn't want to come with me. I ended up flying home a day early, but when I got home, he said he was going to a guys' steak dinner. He didn't get home until 6:00 a.m., when he told me he didn't love me anymore. He said he was no longer attracted to me, and it was over.

The first thing I did, if you can believe it, was tell him to call his mom because I knew she was planning to buy an outfit that day for the wedding. I didn't want her to waste money. Next, I went upstairs and moved him into the other bedroom. Then I drove to my parents house and waited for them to get home.

He ended up staying in the house until it was sold. That was around the time his best friend called me to share that he had been cheating on me. Even though I had found myself at raves and was learning to value myself, I still didn't have enough self-worth to be able to recognize what was and wasn't right for me. He had told me one time that I disgusted him in bed! And I stuck around. That scarred me for a very long time. But his karma came back.

This is not solely my story to tell, but let's just say that he had me over one night, begging me to come back but while showing all his true colors. I left and never looked back. His infidelity was ultimately a blessing, because we had no business being together. We were so young. Anyway, I think I would've seen it coming if I had been better able to value myself at the time.

We don't start out being incapable of valuing ourselves. We're born with a sense of curiosity, which is a component of valuing yourself: curiosity is basically a way of feeling good enough about yourself to go out and explore, try different things, and succeed. But then, as we age, we start questioning ourselves, wondering if we're good enough.

We respond to circumstances. There are big ones, such as, for me, trauma, bullying, and abandonment. After my parents and I decided I would stay in Vancouver, I lived with a grandmother who ended up being unable to care for me—who didn't think I was enough just as her grandchild. I already believed that about myself. Having it modeled for me further only strengthened my belief.

Smaller everyday circumstances pile up too. All of the little things that happen that lead us to second-guess and question ourselves, wonder if we're good enough, and feel small. We lose that propulsive curiosity we were born with. We quiet ourselves. Eventually, we can become doormats—and believe life is *supposed* to be like that. We can get so deep inside of that feeling that we don't know how to change it. We don't even recognize what's happening.

Imagine that you go see a nutritionist. She does a bunch of tests and learns that your cortisol is high and you're slightly intolerant to milk. She recommends a new diet and some supplements, and within a couple of weeks you feel amazing. You didn't even know it was possible to feel that way. You didn't realize how sluggish and uncomfortable you'd previously been. That's what it's like when you devalue yourself your whole life and then suddenly find a community that values you: you recognize what has been happening, and you see a pathway out.

> **SEEING THAT OTHER PEOPLE VALUED ME JUST FOR SHOWING UP ALLOWED ME TO START VALUING MYSELF.**

When I walked into a rave, everyone there was so happy to see me. I didn't have to *do* anything. I didn't have to perform or trade something in exchange for their love. I just showed up in my fifty-inch pants, my little crop top, my baseball bat with the stars and trinkets on it, and my *Lion King* backpack, and they ran up to give me hugs. Seeing that other people valued me just for showing up allowed me to start valuing myself. That gave me energy, pep in my step.

Suddenly, I was excited to get up in the morning. I felt on top of the world. So I kept raving. And I continued learning to value myself. I started to feel strong and motivated, and I was able to see the trauma I had experienced. I thought, *These people who barely know me are happy to see me—why didn't my grandmother even bother to say hello when I came home from school?* Why did she not want to care for me when I was on my own?

I started to see that that behavior was more about her than it was about me. That she wasn't happy with herself and took that out on me. Or at least, that was my suspicion. To be fair, I didn't ask. I was young and didn't feel it was my place with an elder. Also, honestly, I don't think I had the awareness at that age to be capable of having a conversation like that, a conversation that's ultimately about generational trauma. That awareness, I developed later (and we'll get to later).

Once I started valuing myself, I trusted myself. And I started to find my voice, not just through screaming plays on the softball field but through the confidence to speak up and share my perspective and thoughts on different things, whether at work or in a difficult conversation with my family. Every time I did that, I got a little bit stronger; I found another piece in the puzzle of self-worth.

When I do speak my mind, it usually puts a microscope over whomever I'm talking to. People who have done the work, are on their own path to self-worth, and who understand themselves will listen to me, provide a safe and positive space, and be confident in what they share as well. On the other hand, people who haven't done the work and aren't on a journey to self-worth tend to get uncomfortable when I use my voice or profess my worth. They create a negative space. You can feel the friction right away. Honestly, I think I scare them a little bit. Since I've learned to assert my values and speak my peace, I've been able to develop much stronger relationships.

Very few friendships have stuck with me from early in my life. Yes, I moved around a lot. But I think that's mostly because my previous relationships were developed at a time when I didn't value myself. There I go blaming myself...again. Now that I'm an adult and better understand how relationships work, I know that there are so many outside circumstances affecting a friendship that have nothing to do with the two people in it.

In my youth, I focused *only* on the people—and blamed one or the other of them. I either blamed myself for being unlikable or incapable, or I blamed the other person for not putting in enough effort. But there are so many outside factors that we forget or don't know about. In reality, you never know what's going on in someone's life (not least your own!).

Before, I was often just looking for external validation. I was struggling to understand who I was and what I gave to the world. So I would give, give, give, give, give. And then people would take. They walked all over me, and I'd be left alone again.

I had to learn that the validation needs to come mostly from within. I had to get my own shit together before I could pour into somebody else's cup. I'm still learning this! I do not have this down 100 percent. I struggle with it sometimes. But I remind myself that even though it's important to consider other people's perspectives and opinions, I can't give too much weight to their opinions about me. Validation has to come from me as well.

WHEN YOU KNOW YOUR OWN WORTH, YOU WON'T GIVE IT AWAY.

Still, it's OK to get affirmation from others—that's just how we're built as humans, and anyway, sometimes that's how the process begins. But you have to actually show up for *yourself* on a daily basis. Only then can you understand the impact you make on the world. Life is a series of choices. If you are in a relationship, you wake up and choose your partner every day (or not). You choose to work out and work toward your health and well-being. You choose how often to reach out and call someone you love. These choices not only shape who we are but are also indications of what we value and how much effort we will put into something or someone.

When you know your own worth, you won't give it away. If somebody questions it, you can answer honestly rather than get emotional. Because people *will* question your worth—on a daily basis. Especially if you're an entrepreneur: "We don't want to spend that kind of money on your service." Or maybe you're negotiating a salary and hear "You're not worth that kind of money."

Usually, once you start valuing yourself, other people will as well. But it's also possible they won't. Sometimes you're the *only* person you can count on. And we have to be OK with that. Even if I'm the only person who values me, that's OK.

Like I said, I still struggle with this. To a certain degree, I'll always seek outside validation because I work online creating content. If only for the fact that I need engagement with that content in order for my business to thrive, I have to seek outside validation. The challenge is to try not to get sucked into comparison. I see someone else doing something I like and I spiral. I think, *Why aren't we doing that? I need to do more even though I'm completely burned out and can't do more.*

I also sometimes struggle with feelings I have about my advocacy work around women in the industry and through my *Blended* podcast, which I launched in 2020 out of a desire to talk more about inclusion in the workplace. I pour time and money into building membership groups and trying to grow communities, but they don't always grow as fast as I'd like. Meanwhile, I see other groups—especially the free ones—getting traction and growing. I start to feel like I'm not doing enough. I get upset and I start to think, *Gosh, I was hoping this effort would give me more back.* And then I realize that's kind of self-serving and not the point of advocacy—which makes me think I've tied my advocacy to my self-worth.

I have to remind myself that advocacy is not about one person or one organization; it's about the people we serve. There is too much ego in advocacy, especially when it comes to women's initiatives. It's no wonder pay equity is going to take another 140 years when we don't collaborate and bring everyone together. Instead, we spread each other thin with time, money, energy, and resources.

There have been times over the last few years when another group did better than mine, and I thought, *Did I not do enough for the community? Do they not see the value? Is that why they're not supporting me in the ways I need—financially or otherwise?* In such a moment, I have to catch myself, check my motives and recalibrate around my "why."

It's OK to have desperate thoughts like that. You're human. You're not going to be a saint all the time. These thoughts come in. The key is to reframe them so you don't tie your advocacy to your self-worth. You don't want to feel bad about yourself just because your expectations—however human—aren't being met.

If you've ever felt left out, or if someone doesn't respond fast enough, it's easy to feel like that's a reflection on you. Like, *What did I do wrong? Are they mad at me?* We obsess over conversations, ruminate. But the responses of other people do not measure your worth. When you catch yourself questioning your motives, ask: What's the root of this? What's beneath this feeling of disappointment or selfishness? Maybe it's because you've tied it to your self-worth. Then just shift your perspective. Look at it from a different angle.

When we step back, we realize we don't have control over other people's actions. What we do have control over is how we respond, how we feel about ourselves. That should be the north star of self-worth.

I definitely still base a lot of my self-worth on how others respond to me—and that's got to be because I was bullied as a kid. I didn't feel like I was good enough. People didn't like me. Even a lack of response triggered those feelings. So every day I fight not to let engagement or outside validation be my only "why." I remind myself that I do what I do in order to create safe spaces and make an impact in that way.

I don't want to put up more content that's just part of the noise. I want to create content that matters, whether that's giving a new founder a platform to tell their story or bringing people together in a safe space so they can authentically share their stories. I remind myself that I've built credibility within the industry, and people trust me with their brands, executives, and stories and to put out quality content. But that's taken a long time, almost eight years to build.

Somebody told me the other day that I'm like the drum beat of the industry: I show up when I say I will, do the things I say I'll do, and create reliable content. That might sound boring to a lot of people, but to me it's cool. It was a huge compliment.

Remember that energy healer I mentioned? The one who told me that my personal life has been messy specifically so that I could learn the lessons necessary to now create safe spaces for other people. First of all, talk about valuing yourself: she wasn't cheap. She charged so much, she definitely values herself. And she should.

I took about two pages of notes, and they've become something I reference on a regular basis. I read them sometimes before I go to bed at night just to remind me. She also told me I'm the only person who can do what I do, which has been a hugely helpful reminder. I do see that in my work and believe that about myself, *and* it's nice to have it validated back to me.

But I mostly remind myself what she said about my ability to create safe spaces. We can turn our struggles into superpowers. I don't think I would be as good at helping people share their perspectives and feel seen and heard—and I certainly wouldn't be *driven* to do so—if I hadn't previously struggled with just those things. Now, when I have a hard time in my personal life, instead of asking myself, *Why is this so hard? Why is it always me?* I instead see the struggle as fueling my superpower.

I recognize that the more I understand myself and work to make myself seen and heard, the better able I'll be to help somebody else feel seen and heard. And truly, that's the point. If no one listens to any episodes of *Blended,* I would still be happy that I had created space for respectful dialogue around hard topics that give people opportunities to speak their minds. But of course, people are listening.

Hey, you don't have to go to an energy healer to get information about yourself. Everywhere around you are nuggets of validation that will help you start finding it within yourself. The more you share yourself and speak up, whether to partners, close friends, colleagues, or people you meet at cocktail parties, the more you'll get back about yourself and your worth, the more you'll be able to keep building it from within.

Not everything the universe sends your way will be good advice. But if it resonates with you and gives you some sort of clarity about something you've been questioning, then it's a download from the universe to pay attention to. It's a message that you can find bravery in the brokenness.

CHAPTER 3

SHINE WITHOUT APOLOGY

WHEN I WAS WORKING AS A TRAFFIC COORDINATOR AT MY parents' company, I attended operations meetings. The whole department would be in the conference room, maybe fifteen of us. At the beginning of one of these meetings, the VP of operations walked in and told everyone they should be careful and stop talking because I would go home and tell my parents everything they said. To single me out in front of the whole room for any reason was embarrassing enough, but to paint me as some kind of spy or tattletale, even if jokingly, was even worse. And yet, even if I was mortified, I wasn't shocked. I just stared at him. By that point I was used to it. I expected that kind of treatment.

Still, I didn't know how to respond. If I said, "No, I won't," I'd play into his hand, and anyway, responding that way would definitely make it sound like I *was* reporting back to my parents. But, on the other hand, if I played along by replying, "Oh, we've got the whole room bugged anyway," I'd be just as unprofessional as he was. So not only was it a rude, unfair, and belittling slight—disguised as a quote-unquote joke—but it put me in the uncomfortable position of either stooping to his level or proving him right. So I did nothing. I held it together through the rest of the meeting and then went to the bathroom to cry.

That VP was the same guy who used to joke that I kept ecstasy in my desk drawer. Clearly, he was a bit of a dick.

I guess from the outside it seemed like a great job to work for your parents and move your way up the ladder. But I was between a rock and a hard place—and pressured from both sides. My parents didn't want to look like they gave me special treatment, but people assumed I was getting special treatment regardless. Since people were suspicious that I didn't deserve my job, I was eager to prove myself, which often led to me being taken advantage of when people dumped extra work on me.

Nobody ever recognized the twelve-hour days or that I completed two times more work than anybody else in my department. Plus, it was a different time; there were no discussions around mental health or burnout.

Looking back, I can see that my self-worth was tied to performance. I knew I would take over the company one day, so I was willing to do as much work as possible. Even if nobody acknowledged how hard I worked, I just told myself, *One day I'd be in charge, and then, I'll have more say and control.*

I never knew whom I could trust. I never knew why somebody was talking to me—if they were pumping me for information or looking for something they could share with other people. Did they want to tear me down or further their own career by being close with the bosses' daughter or having the inside scoop? To be sure, it was also a cool gig, and I got great opportunities—but I did work hard for those opportunities, and, looking back, I felt my work didn't get the recognition it deserved.

For me, working in a family business was lonely. Honestly, I cried a lot those days. More often than not, people violated my trust. I often heard things that had been said about me behind my back. And I started having panic attacks. I had just come off of all that shit in Vancouver, only to walk into a whole new form of bullying.

I don't tell you all of this to say, "Oh, woe is me." I hear from people every day who feel they aren't taken seriously in the workplace. Usually, it's women. Back when I started working at my parents' company, it was a time when men were not very nice in the workplace. I don't want to pretend like it hasn't gotten better, twenty-five years later, because it has. But it does persist. And even if it didn't, most of us are still dealing with trauma from the past. I had a conversation with someone who said she's always the one who's expected to get tea for meetings, who's automatically assumed to be the one to take notes.

Women are helpful. That's not necessarily a bad thing. Especially because we often derive some amount of self-worth from being helpful or doing the right thing. But, at the same time, that helpful impulse diminishes our value in other people's minds. Quote-unquote helpful acts of service are not always valued much in the workplace, if they are recognized at all. Worse, when we internalize that helpful acts of service are women's work and less valuable work, women fail to support one another at the office.

When I was in grade school, there was a neighbor girl who would play with me on our street in the afternoons but then bully me at school. That's what it feels like sometimes between women in the workplace: they cheer on one another in society in general but can't do the same in the conference room or by the water cooler.

I had a recent discussion about competition at one of my dinners in Vegas for women in supply chain. This was a younger generation of professionals—women in their thirties and forties—talking about how they came up at a time when there was usually only room for one woman in a position of power in any given department. That created a competition among them, which led to suspicion and minimized support. A guest on my podcast, who was at the top of her game at Home Depot, once told me the one thing she regrets in her career is that she had not more often reached down to pull other women up. A lot of women in their thirties and forties told me they empathized with her statement because that's just the way it was back then.

But not now. Now there's more room for collaboration and empowerment. More opportunity to say somebody else's name in a room. And more freedom to shout our own names without fear of cultural retribution. Still, old habits are hard to break. The women I feature in my supply-chain series usually decline to share their blog, podcast, or socials because they don't want to sound like they're bragging.

On the other end of the spectrum, I've noticed that women don't as often comment on and repost other women who are featured on the podcast. I don't know. I've had a lot of conversations to try to figure it out, and I still can't. But I do think it's an example of how, as women, we get in our own way. No wonder it's taking us forever to move to parity when we don't necessarily support each other's achievements publicly.

While I'm on the subject, I also wish we'd create fewer women's groups. That's not a misprint. When so many great female-forward organizations already exist, why not put our money and resources behind those and collectively push forward a movement that already has momentum? When we keep starting from scratch, we divide everyone's energy. No wonder it's taking us so long.

Some days, I get a message from someone saying the *Women in Supply Chain* series inspired her, or I hear from a former guest about how much attention she got from the show. On other days, I see someone post, "You know what we don't have in this industry? A series about women in supply chain!" And it gets 400 reactions and 150 comments before anyone tags me. Sometimes I think it's easier to cry, "Shame!" about a supposed lack than it is to research what's already out there and then support whoever's doing the work.

Sometimes we work at cross purposes like this simply out of naivety. Someone wants to launch a new group or vehicle simply because she doesn't realize it already exists or thinks more groups means more opportunity to do good. Other times, people want to create their own vehicle in order to get attention and notoriety. Either way, it rarely does much good and instead pulls us in different directions.

Another misconception concerns free groups. People might think they're making networking or leadership organizations more accessible by making them free. What they're actually doing is diminishing other women who are doing something similar but value their time and expertise enough to charge for it. Often people will justify running a free membership group by saying they want to be inclusive. But charging people fees so you can pay for production and admin does not mean you're not being inclusive. For example, 95 percent of my team are freelancers who are essentially women-owned businesses. I have to charge for my groups so that I can pay them their worth. The money grows ten fold in the community when we invest in each other.

> **DOING THINGS FOR FREE AS A WOMAN PERPETUATES THE STORYLINE THAT WOMEN WILL DO THINGS FOR FREE.**

If someone comes to you and says, "I can't afford the membership," that's when you can decide whether or not to give it to them for free or at a discount. The other thing is that when people don't pay, they don't have skin in the game, and they won't show up to your virtual events or participate in the group—and that participation is exactly what makes the group valuable to everyone else in it. Anyway, doing things for free as a woman perpetuates the storyline that women will do things for free (like, ahem, getting tea or taking notes).

Before launching anything, research who's already working in that space. Wherever you see a gap, absolutely work to fill it in. Perhaps talk with existing leaders adjacent to that space about collaborating on your idea rather than starting a competing organization. Maybe they'll even pay you to do it.

Self-worth is definitely tied to financial worth. Partly that's determined by how you define success. Is it an amount of money? Having a house? Having cars? If you're not making money by whatever age you decided you *should* be making money, you'll start feeling bad about yourself. And then when you negotiate a contract or salary, those down feelings will affect how you represent yourself. Most women undervalue themselves in these scenarios. They aren't comfortable charging much for their services or asking for a higher salary.

Sometimes I do it too! It took me a long time to value my services. When I finally got a director role while working for my parents, my superior was appalled by my salary and made sure I received at least the minimum base salary for a director role. He was actually the driving force behind me starting to see my value and get paid for my work. I was thirty-five then!

It took me a long, long, long, *long* time. Once I was out on my own, I carried that force with me and chose to practice valuing myself monetarily. What worked for me was to increase the price of each service by a little every year. I had to test out what price points would actually fly. Then I got a business coach, and I increased it by a *lot* more because he advised me to. (By the way, it took me a year to say yes to the investment of getting a business coach. Because the investment scared me. I should have done it sooner.)

When I started the podcast, I was charging $100 an episode, which didn't cover anything but the editing. I paid most of my expenses out-of-pocket. Eventually, I realized that the fee I charged guests was really just a business expense. My fees were paid by the corporate offices of wherever my guests worked. Over time, I got to the point where I was charging $500 an episode. Then, someone who came on the show said he would've paid

$1,000. That was the day I started charging $1,000. There have been increases since. About every six months I change my price. Note that the boss, business coach, and guest I've just mentioned are all men.

When I was underpaid at my parents' company, in my twisted mind, I thought, *I'm saving the company money. I'm making a sacrifice for the greater good*. Another way of saying this is that I thought I was being *helpful*. These are the excuses we invent to explain away suspicions that we aren't actually being taken care of. And that doesn't just happen to women. We all do it.

I was an A+ student at it, always making excuses for a variety of things. I certainly did it with my first boyfriend and my fiancé. That kind of distorted thinking is part of what got me through. I created scenarios in order to keep myself from getting lost. But the reality is that people show you who they are. Believe them.

That said, there's a fine line between advocating for yourself and valuing yourself on the one hand and then on the other hand, expecting more from someone than that person might be interested in or willing to give you. For example, I once had a team member complain that he had put so much money and extra effort into the company, and I had not paid him in kind for it or showed enough appreciation. But I had not asked him to do any of that. Honestly, I didn't want him to do it. And now I was being made to feel responsible. Anyway, I had said the words *I appreciate it* and *thank you very much* several times, but it wasn't enough. Honestly, I felt gaslighted.

The exchanges clearly indicated how he felt about himself at the time, about his self-worth and how he valued himself. That wasn't advocating for himself as much as it was posturing. I've fallen into this trap myself at times, when I went above and beyond for people specifically because I didn't feel good about myself. And then I became angry when they didn't respond the way I wanted them to. It can become a vicious cycle because then you feel unappreciated and even worse about yourself. This can turn into another form of self-sabotage when you keep setting the bar unrealistically high, and then no one can provide you with the amount of appreciation you believe you deserve. When you constantly feel like everyone's disappointing you, you can't leave room for relationships to grow.

But when you *are* being undervalued, that's a different story. In such a circumstance, it can be easier to make excuses than face the truth of what's happening, especially if you're being bullied or taken advantage of. It's hard work to go through your feelings and sort out reality. If you've had drama like I went through with my childhood bullying, you end up believing that poor treatment from other people is your natural state of life. People stay in abusive relationships because they make up excuses for why it won't happen again. They make up excuses about the other person because they feel like abuse is what they deserve.

> **ENDLESS SELF-IMPROVEMENT CAN BE A WAY TO MASK THAT YOU DON'T THINK IT'S ENOUGH JUST TO BE YOURSELF.**

It's not only trauma that leads to distorted thinking. I see it also in my own compulsion to always be bigger and better. Somebody told me once that I used to be a serial seminar attendee because I hit up so many conferences and seminars while I was working for my parent's company. I've always wanted to do more, learn more, get better, be better. But I have to be careful because you can get trapped in that. Endless self-improvement can be a way to mask that you don't think it's enough just to be yourself. And it can be an excuse to avoid doing the work on yourself that really needs your attention.

One way to break free of that distortion is to celebrate your wins. It's part of the self-worth journey and process to give yourself space to celebrate. And it can be small wins—maybe you actually finished your to-do list for the day. Honestly, I'm still working on this. I don't always actually stop to acknowledge success when it happens. But I am getting better.

For example, one time I was honored at an event in New York City hosted by one of the *Real Housewives of Beverly Hills*. Twelve of my friends came. Just to celebrate me. Some of them even flew in for it. I'm usually the type of person who doesn't even tell anyone about accolades, but I had decided to put it out there, and the response of support was beautifully overwhelming.

Still, I knew I'd feel guilty, so I forced myself to lean in: I asserted boundaries and said, "If you're going to come, come for me, not just to meet the celebrity. This is to celebrate something special for me." Then I announced that I had planned some glam for us. We were going to get our hair and makeup done. It felt incredible to know that my friends wanted to come, even though it was just going to be about me. They legitimately wanted to support me.

Several times over the weekend, I was struck with guilt anyway. I thought, *Oh my God, these people spent all this money to be here. I hope they feel like it's worth it.* But I was able to quiet that voice and remind myself that they wanted to be there and I didn't have to worry about them. They made the choice to celebrate me because I'm worth celebrating.

AFFECTION ISN'T PERFORMANCE-BASED.

Women often feel that we have to *do* something in order to receive love and acceptance. We feel worth is based on performance: what we do for other people, our kids, our spouses. When in reality, if you're in the right space with the right people, you shouldn't have to do anything to be accepted. Affection isn't performance-based.

I am certain that my inspiration to create the *Women in Supply Chain* series was born during my time working for my parents' company. Ditto for the advocacy work I do around that for my *Blended* series and for my nonprofit, Blended Pledge, which provides grants for travel expenses so diverse voices can accept invitations to speaking engagements (and, as a result, supports more inclusion on industry stages). My reasons for creating these entities were partly selfish: I wanted to find my voice. I wanted to create a platform to celebrate other women's voices because the role models I'd had throughout my career up until that point, other than my mom, didn't really inspire me. Through advocacy work and creating a platform on which to hear other people's stories, I came to understand the value of my own story. It helped me to see myself in others. And I believe it's helping my listeners as well.

Not every journey is the same. Yours might not look like everyone else's. It certainly won't be straight. For example, when you hear other people's stories, you realize that if you haven't done all the things by thirty-five, you're actually on track because, based on my guests, most people don't really start achieving until their forties. This all builds self-worth, knowing we're not alone, hearing about the good, the bad, and the ugly in everyone else too, especially in our role models.

I told you that I believe my personal life has been messy in order to help me build safe spaces for others. Honestly, my personal life is still fairly messy. I'm able to make sense of that through my journey into advocacy. Learning people's stories, especially those of women and people of color, helps me connect to my superpower, helps me truly believe in the work I do to create opportunities to collaborate with and celebrate one another. Through the advocacy, I've learned how important it really is to feel seen and heard. All I have to do is give people a platform to be exactly who they are—whether I or anyone else thinks they're right, wrong, or indifferent.

The greatest gift we can give someone is to let them feel seen and heard, to shine their light unapologetically. I spent a lot of my life hiding my light. Now I'm shining it, and I hope this gives you permission to do the same. I hope you never feel the need to hide your light—whether that's because you think someone doesn't value it or doesn't want to see it. But if you do, remember that as long as *you* value it, others will too. Shine on.

CHAPTER 4

EVERYONE DOUBTS; NOT EVERYONE QUITS

ONE DAY, WHEN I WAS NINETEEN, WHILE GETTING IN THE car, as I reached for the door handle, I fainted. I just fell to the ground. It was the first time I had ever fainted. My boyfriend and friends gathered around me. I woke up right away. They got me into the car and took me home. I was so embarrassed, thinking, *What's wrong with me?* and *Now I'm a burden on everybody else*. From that day forward, I started having panic attacks.

Whenever I was tired or feeling anxiety over something—maybe a conversation that had felt a bit aggressive or combative—my blood pressure would drop, I'd feel hot or just uncomfortable, or I'd get ringing in my ears. And then sometimes, I would have a panic attack. They happened in a variety of environments and scenarios. They even came on at work. I'd go into my mom's office and ask her to talk to me because then I could normalize what was happening, convince myself I was in a safe space, and return to work.

I once had a panic attack while flying to Helsinki. I was connecting in Frankfurt, Germany. I was exhausted because I don't sleep well on planes, and it had been an overnight flight. So I was rundown in the Frankfurt airport, and suddenly I was having a panic attack. In a moment like that, the world kind of distorts—my ears start ringing, my heart races, my blood pressure plummets, and then I feel like I'm going to faint. After pacing the airport and willing myself not to faint by trying to convince myself I was safe, I bought a drink with electrolytes in it, then went into the bathroom and, while sitting on a toilet, called my husband and asked him to calm me down.

PART OF SELF-WORTH IS NOT TRYING TO DO EVERYTHING YOURSELF.

In the moment of a panic attack, I feel an immense amount of shame. I think, *Why can't I get my shit together?* My therapist and I discussed the importance of having a safe space during an attack, having someone I can turn to who can help me through it so I won't be alone. That experience of pushing through shame in order to ask someone I trust for help was extremely good for my self-worth. Part of self-worth is not trying to do everything yourself but understanding who your safe connections are and being able to reach for them.

We *try* to do everything ourselves. We can't do everything ourselves. Part of being kind to yourself is understanding your limits and removing judgment from the act of seeking help. If, during a panic attack, I was to go to someone who was not a safe space, that does me a disservice because I wouldn't be putting myself in the best possible position. The shame would actually grow. But when you ask for help, you actually put yourself first, and when you ask someone you trust, you also put yourself first in a space where it's possible to feel whatever it is you need to feel. For me, that process diminished my shame and helped me prioritize myself in moments when I really needed to.

Those early panic attacks were consumed by shame. I eventually realized they were even triggered by it. They always occurred when I felt faint. But that wasn't just a physical symptom. To me, fainting was humiliating. It made me feel silly. And vulnerable. Like I didn't have it all together. It felt like an outward sign of my inability to care for myself. And I hated that it meant somebody had to help me, that I was a burden on everybody else.

The thought of fainting in a public space made me panic. I hated having eyes on me, especially during public speaking. I experienced panic attacks randomly and periodically until I was about twenty-six or twenty-seven. Sometimes they came back to back, like every couple of weeks. Sometimes as many as six months would pass between them.

They happened at work, they happened at home, they happened in public with lots of people around. I got good at hiding them. Only a few people knew, whomever I felt safe telling. Otherwise, I rode them out, pretended they weren't happening, or found a bathroom stall to sit in until they passed.

In my early thirties, they slowed down to maybe once a year. But then they came back around forty-two, after I had my first surgery for lipedema. I didn't give myself enough time to rest before going back to work. I had an attack, and then they started occurring more regularly again. The difference this time around is that I didn't have that safe space I required. There was no one I could turn to to hold my hand or talk through it with me—because the attacks started happening while I was onstage, live on camera, or in the middle of a podcast recording.

Anyone watching or listening would have no idea. I've always felt the show must go on. So I summoned all my focus in that moment to get through the conversation. I would never stop a show, even when I have an overwhelming feeling of panic. So I keep talking or moderating.

But in my head, I'm coaching myself to get through. Then, as soon as I end the live show or walk off stage, I cry or collapse in exhaustion. It takes everything out of me: not just a panic attack but the focus to carry on through it. If I'm onstage, I'll usually find a safe person afterward whom I can tell what happened, just to make sure no one had noticed.

I once emceed an annual general meeting for a large steamship line and had several panic attacks throughout the day. It was the first time I'd done anything like that. Of course, the night before, I had gotten maybe two hours of sleep. So I was already a little bit on edge because sleep deprivation is one of the triggers for my panic attacks. And then I had to be onstage on and off for seven hours. The event was in a beautiful old museum in Hamburg, Germany. And the ceiling was all glass, meaning the sun came streaming through in the afternoon, right onto me. Being hot is yet another trigger. I thought, *This is a perfect storm*.

I was standing there, moderating a great panel discussion, when all of a sudden, I had this overwhelming feeling I was about to faint. I could feel my blood pressure dropping. I started strategically taking little sips of water to help me focus on something. (That's my tell: drinking water. It gives me something to *do*. If you see me drinking a lot of water onstage, it means I'm having a panic attack.) I listened. I looked at my iPad. I took a sip of water. I asked the next question from my script. I just kept going. And then it happened again during the next panel discussion. This was the first time I'd experienced them at an in-person event.

After the whole thing was said and done, I was honestly pretty proud of myself. First, I had never done a gig like that before. Second, I cannot memorize anything, and they didn't have a teleprompter, so I figured out how to get a teleprompter on my laptop. And most important, I had pushed through the attack instead of letting it derail me. For the first time ever, I didn't feel ashamed afterward. I started talking about it right away. Not long after, I experienced an attack during a live podcast stream, and as soon as we stopped the live stream, I told everyone what had happened and how I felt.

In general, I started talking about them more than I had when they were happening in my twenties. I think, all those years later, I had simply become a different person. The second time around, I had more confidence, more self-worth. I didn't feel I needed to hide the panic attacks. I felt it was important to talk about them, not only for me but to normalize it for anyone else facing the same struggle. If these are real for me, they probably are for many other people.

I also started talking more about my mental health. I don't experience as much shame around mental health and anxiety now. If somebody else is having anxiety or panic attacks or is afraid to speak onstage because of that, I want to make sure I do whatever I can to support them through it. I want us all to accept it as normal and not hide behind it anymore.

But my path is not necessarily your path. What's good for me isn't necessarily good for you. If sharing your panic attacks feels even scarier than having them, then you need to make the choice that feels good to you. Honestly, most of the time the people around you aren't even paying enough attention to notice what's going on with you. So whether you share your struggle or not, there's no need to exist in a shame bubble about your anxiety when you're the only one who knows about it! That doesn't mean those around you don't care about you; it just means they don't see your anxiety.

Being nervous is a normal part of everyday life. Panic attacks are just one way your body gets through an anxious episode. If it happens to everyone in a variety of ways, why shouldn't it be normal? People don't need to be ashamed of it or try to hide it behind who they think they need to or should be.

I wish I could say that after I started normalizing my panic attacks, they eased up. But no. I even started having them during softball, which was weird because that's always been my safe space, something I've done for more than thirty years. But then I experienced an episode during an inning. I called my brother-in-law over to sit with me.

We walked away from the dugout, and I said, "I need you. I'm having a panic attack. I need you to talk to me." I started crying because it scared me that something I've been doing for so long and felt so comfortable with could have triggered an attack. After that, I probably had one or two a season. I'm now contemplating switching out of a competitive level to see if that helps.

But I will say that, now, during my second phase of living with panic attacks, I do at least feel better equipped to deal with them. Sharing my reality with others has given me the confidence and courage to handle it all moment to moment. We really don't talk about it enough. We acknowledge that public speaking is a big fear, but we don't discuss specifically why and what comes up around it. We expect executives, professionals, and leaders to be OK taking the stage in front of five thousand people, like it's supposed to be totally natural for them, rather than allowing them to be like the rest of us. I don't think that's fair. We should go easier both on ourselves and on others.

And we should make space to talk about the anxieties of public speaking and about panic attacks in general. Otherwise, when people panic, they might believe they're not good enough to be on that stage or good enough to have their title. How can you build self-worth and confidence if you're constantly hiding the truth of your experience? Your fears don't have to define you, but you should have the opportunity to speak about them candidly, especially because then your teams can learn from that.

And you can better manage it when you're not trying to hide it. When we tell ourselves simply to handle something hard without exploring or expressing why it's hard, we're not actually solving a problem but making it worse. Talking about it helps problem-solve it, helps us all learn from each other, and makes us all feel less alone.

Fortunately, with my own issues, there *has* been some improvement. I have blessedly lost the second-level panic, meaning I no longer have attacks *about* having attacks. (Previously, a week before an onstage event, I'd start panicking out of fear that I'd have an episode.)

I've also started listening to the panic attacks, trying to understand them as warning signs. They're ultimately part of the fight-or-flight response. When I got them during softball, I considered that I might be pushing myself too hard or that maybe it was time to play in a less rigorous league. When I get them on the job, I look for stressors that can be avoided.

I've figured out how to sleep better during the nights before any kind of event that typically triggers an attack. I bought a white-noise machine and a weighted blanket for my eyes called a NodPod. Sometimes I take a sleep supplement. And I focus on my nutrition and get nutrient IVs a week before I travel. Doing everything possible to stay healthy enough to avoid an attack has helped—and so has *knowing* I'm doing everything possible.

WHEN WE NORMALIZE ANXIETY, WE TAKE THE SHAME OUT OF IT.

I'm also learning how to sit with it. I tell myself, *Oh, I'm just having a panic attack. It's all good. I'm safe onstage, and we're having a conversation. And I can let it flow through me.* It's taken a while to get here. And it began with me just wanting to normalize it for myself. When we do so, we take the shame out of anxiety, and then we aren't thinking about ourselves so poorly.

Still, I do try to talk about them, when they're happening or otherwise. Because the more I talk about it, the more my listeners believe they can also get to a place where they can sit with their panic attacks and let them flow through. They see that I don't let my panic attacks hold me back and realize theirs don't have to hold them back either.

Finally, I started reciting a daily affirmation. I've printed it for you below, in case you can pull anything helpful from it. Every morning, while I walk the dogs, I recite it. (Yes, it took me forever to memorize the whole thing.) The affirmation calms me, centers me, and reminds me of not only what I'm grateful for but what I'm capable of. It helps keep the panic attacks at bay. Whenever I feel doubt, it reminds me not to quit.

Some of what's below is from my own brain, but most of it is a hodgepodge of quotes from other people that I've collected over the years and made my own. I could never remember or trace whom to cite. (If you recognize anything in here, let me know, and I'll post the attribution on my website or LinkedIn!) I do at least remember that the last line comes from Tyler Perry.

> Thank you, God and the universe, for this breath on such an amazing day on this incredible journey.

> I am truly grateful for the clothes on our backs, the food on our plates, and the roof over our heads.

> Money flows freely and easily, and I am truly grateful for the money that we have.

> I am beautiful, I am kind, and I am loving. I am a human being with a life of value. Others' opinions of me belong to them, and I will not react to them. I will treat everyone I meet with kindness, respect, love, and peace.

> I believe that everything happens for a reason, I believe that anything is possible, and I believe that I can do anything I put my mind to.

> I believe that I live in the abundance of peace, love, and happiness. I

believe that I live in the abundance of courage and confidence, purpose, worth, greatness, and opportunity.

I believe that I am amazing, I am kind, I am loving and loved, and I am respectful and respected.

I believe that I am making a difference in people's lives and the world. And I believe that I am what a woman who builds a $50 million business looks like.

I believe that I am courageous and confident.

I believe that I am a leader and a public speaker.

I believe that I am worthy of greatness and belong in the rooms with greatness.

I believe that my time is now, and I am ready for the next steps now.

I believe that I am ready for more, ready to make more of a difference in people's lives and the world, and ready to lead a $50 million business. I am ready for more wealth, more success, and more money.

I believe that little miracles happen every day.

CHAPTER 5

BOXES ARE FOR SHIPPING, NOT FOR LIVING

IN FIFTH GRADE, I DID SPEECH COMPETITIONS. I WASN'T scared of speaking in public. One day in school, while preparing for a big competition, my teacher asked me to practice my speech in front of the class. So I got up and said my speech, confident as ever. When I finished, some of the kids in class threw paper balls at me and booed. I blacked out.

My memory's a little fuzzy, but I think I ran to the bathroom. I do remember that the teacher did nothing—she didn't come after me or say anything. Eventually, I just went back to class. It was one of the most scarring days of my life and turned me off of public speaking for what I thought was going to be forever.

I never overcame it, really. I get nervous every time I speak, but I especially did in high school. There were always presentations. I was even in drama, though I have no idea why I chose that elective; I hated being in front of people. But I was able to stick with group projects, instead of doing individual ones, which helped a bit. Somehow, I made it through high school. After that,

I joined the family business, first in reception, then operations, and eventually sales.

At some point in that timeline, my mom started pushing me to go to Toastmasters. She thought I needed to round out my skills and that one day I'd need public speaking. Every time I thought about Toastmasters or picked up the phone to book my spot, my hands would sweat. I couldn't do it. I probably tried five or six times; I just couldn't bring myself to call. Finally, around 2008, I had a light-bulb moment. Some of my friends were models and actors and often talked about their representation. My great idea? I got a talent agent.

I figured, *If she sends me on auditions and makes me practice being in front of the camera, it will help me practice speaking in front of people*. It didn't go down exactly that way. For example, I couldn't memorize lines. I tried! I remember during one audition, there was this line about laundry—just one line—and I kept messing it up.

Another time, I had to pretend to take clothes out of the dryer, but, of course, there was no dryer and no clothes. And I'm not good at pretending. While removing imaginary clothes from a nonexistent dryer, I was supposed to deliver a line. I'm just not coordinated enough for that. The director yelled at me to leave. I was like, "OK, I'm going." It was awful.

I got yelled at a lot during auditions.

But I didn't get upset with myself—because I knew I didn't want to be an actor. The auditions were terrifying, but I kept doing it. Eventually, in 2012, I got a gig *without* having to audition. It was with Denise Richards. At the time, she had a haircare product with her hairstylist. I have really thick hair, so I guess they picked me out of a lineup.

I spent the day on live TV at the Shopping Channel with her. I was so scared, but I did it. I also did a live breakfast TV segment with her. (She was great, had no big entourage, and was very down to earth. She offered to buy us all dinner, so she hopped in my car, and we drove to the restaurant to pick up the food. Everyone wanted photos, so I played photographer.)

After that, I landed a pet-food commercial, an appearance at Walmart's annual general meeting, and a few other things, including a national photography campaign (I got recognized from that one by an old family friend, who reached out to me about it on Facebook, which was fun).

Then, as fate would have it, my parents bought the All About Pets Show. To this day, I'm not sure why. They had a love for horses, and I think they wanted to incorporate that into the show, which was a great idea but in hindsight not our jam. It was a big live expo show in Toronto that happened on Easter weekend. Somehow—I guess because of my crowning achievements with Denise Richards and the Shopping Channel—I ended up as the spokesperson. I appeared on the news three times, once from the show and twice from the newsroom.

The first time, I spoke live with Ann Rohmer, a known figure in the Toronto news, alongside a blind rottweiler and its handler. Unfortunately, I'm terrified of big dogs—just as much as I am of public speaking or being on camera. It was all I could do to not shake on the couch during the segment. When I was younger, I was chased by a pit bull and a Doberman. And then there I was, with this rottweiler at my feet.

My brother, who watched from home, later told me that he was yelling at the TV the whole time, "Pet the damn dog!" There I was, representing the All About Pets Show, unable to engage with the pet. At the end of the segment, I finally put my hand out and patted it.

After that, I had to speak on stage at the All About Pets Show, introducing speakers on different stages. I think my parents just liked to torture me, jk. I was really only doing it for them. I'm a good family trooper. Little did I know that all of that media training would help me with my media company, being in the spotlight, podcasting, and even appearing on Bloomberg and on the BBC twice. It kind of prepared me without me realizing it. (By the way, you will not be surprised to learn that I was so nervous before the Bloomberg appearance that I did not sleep the night before. When I said yes to the invitation, I joked with my team that she "could have left out the part about the two million viewers"—my anxiety was through the roof. But then they liked what I had to say so much that they pushed their commercial break.)

My brief foray into acting and presenting ended around 2014. I had to focus more on the family business. The auditions just became too much: driving downtown, waiting for hours. I couldn't keep doing it. Anyway, I had learned a lot and felt like I didn't need the talent agent anymore. It no longer served me, but it had definitely been valuable.

SOMETIMES YOU REACH YOUR DESTINATION BY TAKING AN ALTERNATIVE PATH.

Although the auditions and appearances gave me a lot of anxiety, at the end of the day, I kept showing up. I didn't say no. I did them, even if I was nervous, and every time, I proved to myself that I could do it. In hindsight, I realize that many of the things I said yes to in my business—especially when I was nervous but did something anyway—only happened because of what I learned from those experiences. Saying yes and doing it anyway became a key part of my mindset. I gained resilience. I learned that I can do things, even if I think I can't. Trying everything at least once is key. You either like it or don't like it, are good at it or not. You have to try things to realize your potential, and I've tried a lot of different things.

Sometimes you reach your destination by taking an alternative path. For public speaking, a traditional path would be Toastmasters. I didn't have formal training. I took an alternative route by getting a talent agent instead. It was my way of tackling the fear of public speaking. I've always carved my own path. When I started my podcast, supply-chain media wasn't even a term. I didn't take a traditional approach, and I don't typically follow the beaten path. (Yes, I now realize that's on trend for me.)

> **TRYING DIFFERENT THINGS HELPS YOU UNDERSTAND OTHER PEOPLE'S EXPERIENCES, AND THAT EMPATHY CREATES A SAFE SPACE.**

This experience of finding an alternative path to overcome fears—of throwing myself into auditions in order to learn public speaking—also helped me develop my superpower. When you try different things, you encounter challenges that help you empathize with others. We see this happen a lot between sales and marketing. When someone from sales spends time in marketing, they understand both fields better. It creates empathy, which leads to better conversations and solutions. Trying different things helps you understand other people's experiences, and that empathy creates a safe space.

Sometimes people describe love as being meant to be, or that two people in a couple were meant to find one another. I feel that way about myself and public speaking. I wonder if, in some way, this was always supposed to be my path. Then the incident in fifth grade, when my classmates threw balls of paper at me, shifted my journey away from that path. But then, my path shifted again back toward it after I thought outside the box and got a talent agent.

That also served as my first actionable step toward getting over my anxiety. When I started getting asked to do speaking engagements or moderate panel discussions, I said yes without hesitation, assuming that I would figure out my anxiety later. What possessed me to say yes, knowing that I'd lose sleep and potentially have a panic attack? Knowing that my life would be turned upside down every time, I kept saying yes anyway. Why? That's what I mean when I say maybe it was meant to be my path. I had a gut feeling. Something in me pushed me forward. Life wouldn't let it go.

When life puts the same thing in front of you over and over again, it's trying to tell you something. Those are moments to try to find a new mindset, to think outside of the box in order to forge a new path—because the world has something big in store for you.

CHAPTER 6

LIFE IS LIVED FORWARD AND UNDERSTOOD BACKWARDS

WHEN YOU'RE WITH SOMEBODY FOR FIVE YEARS, YOU become absorbed into that world. You also get used to having somebody around, to not being alone. But when he one day tells you the engagement is off, when it falls apart and you suddenly find yourself alone, you have choices. You can take some time to get through it—curl up on the couch and cry for days. Or you can go be with other people, do new things, and figure out who you are again. I chose…to do both.

I definitely cried and wallowed for a few days. And then I got off the couch. That's how I ended up in Venice, Italy, on what was supposed to be my wedding day, watching a different couple get married.

It started because I didn't want to be in the country on my botched wedding day. I just didn't. We broke up in April 2003. Now that there wouldn't be a wedding in July, I started researching different things I could do then. I knew I wanted to go to England because I have family there. And then my good friend Lisa, who lives in the UK and is like family, said she would travel with me. She and I had never been on a trip together and chose a package with the organization Contiki Tours.

I spent two weeks with family, and then Lisa and I left London on a bus with a variety of Australians, Americans, and Canadians. The tour covered sixteen countries in thirty days. It was a whirlwind and one of the best things I have ever done. They packed in as many locations as possible. But I wanted to see Europe and didn't want to backpack alone, so I figured this was the safest way.

It started off rocky. Our first stop was Paris, where we stayed in wooden cabins. I'm not a wooden-cabin kind of girl. Then, in the Beaujolais wine region of France, I had to share a bathroom with guys and sleep in bunk beds. Look, I'm not a diva. And at twenty-three, it wasn't *that* bad. But also, I had just been through a lot of trauma. My fiancé came home one day, told me he didn't love me and wasn't attracted to me anymore, and that it was over. Sure, if I really think about it, it was a blessing in disguise. Hindsight is 2020. But still: going through all of that and then a few months later, I'm like, *I'm on this crazy tour bus with people I don't know and sharing bathrooms with strange men.* It felt very different than, say, being on a honeymoon with my new husband.

It wasn't my first travel experience. I had gone somewhere pretty much every year since age eleven. I was very lucky to join my dad on business trips to the UK. I flew back and forth by myself to spend time with my grandparents. But that wasn't necessarily the kind of travel that challenged me. Which is maybe why, on the third day, after waking up in a bunkbed, I thought, *What did I get myself into?* I called Dad and said, "I don't think I can do this." I almost quit. He encouraged me to stay and try it out. I'm so glad I did.

The trip took a turn toward the positive after Lisa and I hooked up with four teachers from Canada. We starting hanging out all the time. It gave us a group of six, so half the group could go one way, half another way. And we all had personalities sort of split down the middle that got along with each other. They were the saving grace. For the rest of the trip, we stuck together on outings and for sleeping arrangements.

First, Paris. Then the Beaujolais wine region. Then Juan-le-Pins. That place was fabulous. They had an open-air market at night, right on the water with all of the yachts and their lights on. Then we went to Nice and also Monaco. The guide said, "We're crossing the border into Monaco. Everybody has to put their passports up against the window." No we didn't—it was a prank. Why is that funny? I don't know. I guess because we all did it? He was like, "You guys will do anything I say." Well yeah, you're the tour operator.

I ended up on the hairpin turn of the Monaco Grand Prix, which was cool. Instead of going to the main casino, we went to one around the corner from it because apparently it was cheaper. We spent eighteen euros on a drink just to say we'd been there.

Next, we visited Jungfrau Mountain in Switzerland. I bought a Swiss watch in Switzerland—I thought that was the coolest thing ever. We went to Lichtenstein just to get our passport stamped to say we'd been there. We went whitewater rafting in the Austrian Alps. The water was freezing. It was terrifying but so much fun. My favorite, favorite place was Vienna, Austria. I shopped my heart out in Vienna and had to ship a box home because I'd bought too much. We drove by an open-air Lady Gaga concert with our bus windows open.

We had big steins of beer in Munich. Then Italy. First Rome, which was a little scary, not gonna lie. But that's also where I experienced one of the highlights of my trip: if you're ever feeling bad about yourself or questioning your self-worth, walk through the Vatican wearing a shirt that says, "If you're cute, I'm single."

Wearing a shirt like that is not something I would typically do. And I hadn't intended to cause a scene. Rather, it was the only thing I had that day that was clean, and I honestly didn't think much of it. It had definitely been a conscious choice to pack the shirt; I was newly single—and in the most brutal way—and thought, *I'm going to pack this and be proud of it and not think too much about it because it's funny.* The fact that I ended up being cat-called in the Vatican was just icing on the cake.

Clearly, I'm not a religious person. (I do have beliefs; they just don't fit any of the traditional molds.) I will say that while I was standing in line to enter, I worried, *What if they don't let me in because of what my T-shirt says?!* I was meeting their dress code by wearing pants and a shawl, but still. And I had nothing else to change into.

But they let me in. And all day, as I walked through the Vatican, the Italian guards shouted, "You're cute! I'm single!" I admit, when I'd put on the shirt, I'd been feeling a bit spicy. But I just thought people would laugh. I didn't know I would get cat-called by the guards. They literally yelled down hallways at me. And I liked it. Those were some really good looking Italian guards at the Vatican. Most people there were getting yelled at for taking pictures. I got called out for a very different reason.

When we left Rome, my group missed the last bus out of the city. So in 40 degree heat (Celsius), we walked back to our—again—wood cabin. By now, you've gathered that I couldn't afford the tour that stayed in hotels.

Then we headed to Florence. I negotiated my way through the markets there, buying different things. It was almost like I was in my element. And I felt my confidence grow. It had been fairly low, for obvious reasons, and I was still trying to find myself. Well, I found myself in a market in Florence.

It was a beautiful day in August. Hot but beautiful. The open-air market was huge. There were stalls for days. I don't know what prompted me, but I started asking questions and trying to negotiate. And it worked. Others from our tour bus heard how I had negotiated prices down and asked, "Can you do it for us?"

It was fun, like a game for me. Everybody won. Everybody was happy afterward. Mostly, I had started doing it because I wanted a lower price on something, but also I wanted to see *what* I could do. I was expanding my horizons, in a way. And I think it also comes down to asking questions—what's the worst that could happen? They could say no. So just ask and try it out. See what happens. Get out of your comfort zone.

To be clear, I was uncomfortable. I was very nervous. I thought, *Who am I and what am I doing?* There was a bit of imposter syndrome, though I did not know that label at that time. And then I was proud of myself for doing it anyway. And I walked away with some pretty cool stuff.

Each time I bargained, I gained a little more confidence. It helped me find my voice on the trip. In the beginning, I was terrified of everything and unsure if this tour was right for me. But in Florence I came into my own. And I learned how to say no to things. Typically, I would go along with the pack just to go along with the pack. But I started to find my voice again in that Florence market, after the trauma of canceling the wedding and everything that came with that—not just the heartbreak but also dealing with vendors, selling the house, and then, of course, having to start over.

Next was Pompeii. That was eye opening because that's the port where all of the seamen dock and then go into Pompeii for food and activities. I didn't realize how prominent sex work was in Pompeii. There were all these rooms with pictures over the doors explaining what happened in each room. Like, specifically.

Then we got on a boat and went to Corfu in Greece. We had a toga party, and I ended up at a water park. Oh, I should say that at the time I was on a mission to try a Big Mac in every country I visited. Greece was probably one of the weirdest ones. I think it came with beer. Not one of my favorites.

Why was this a goal? I don't know. I really liked Big Macs. (This was before I understood my sensitivities to gluten and cheese, and Big Macs were my favorite thing on the face of this planet.) I ate them in Canada, obviously, and then when I visited the UK,

I noticed a difference. I wondered if they would taste different in every country. Incidentally, the best foreign Big Mac was in Korea. That was on a different trip, but if you're curious, I can tell you that it was delivered on a bicycle and didn't have one piece of lettuce out of place. It was picture perfect. I think the worst was in Spain (also a different trip).

Anyway, we were in Greece for a couple of days—it is beautiful and I definitely recommend seeing it. I have been trying to get back, but it hasn't been in the cards yet. Then we took a twenty-four-hour ferry back up Trieste in Italy. Then Venice. I hadn't realized we'd be there on my wedding day. We knew we were doing sixteen countries in thirty days, but I didn't know the itinerary more specifically than that. It was July. Venice can get very smelly in the summer. We stayed in a campground in an RV-type thing, which was perfect (honestly).

And on my wedding day, we went into the city. We had the day to ourselves. The moment we stepped foot into St. Mark's Square, I saw a couple getting married. Right there. On the day I wasn't. I looked to the sky and asked, *Really? The one day I don't wanna see this? When I'm feeling the most vulnerable, you throw a couple in front of me getting married in St. Mark's? Really?!*

Who does that? I still don't know what the hell the universe was telling me that day. Honestly, I think it was just being a jerk.

After wallowing for a moment and witnessing their special moment—I hope they are still madly in love and living their best lives—I went about our business. I actually made a vase out of blown glass that day. We toured a historic jail and rode a gondola, which was not romantic at all. It was me and a bunch of girls on a canal that stank, but it was a great way to see the city.

That night, back at the campground, a bar was set up. People were hanging out and asked me to come along. Instead, I wandered to the shoreline. Lisa went to bed, which hurt me a little, because she knew I was having trouble that day, but I think she was having trouble with the trip in general. I sat by myself, looking out over the water, and all the pent-up emotions from the day came flooding out. I cried and cried.

I cried for the loss. I cried for the future I'd thought I would have. I cried because I was all alone on my wedding day. I cried because I felt like a failure. I cried because I was so far away from everyone who cared about me on a day that was supposed to be one of the happiest of my life. I let it all out. It was so heavy and just what I needed.

Sure, I'd also released some of it by buying a pair of shoes earlier that day. But the raw emotion came out that night by the water. *I was supposed to get married today, and instead I'm in Venice by myself.* I sat with sadness for a while. Then I thought, *But I'm on a beach, and I'm doing cool things. And it's going to be OK.* I cried it out and then met the others at the bar.

I had already shared with quite a few people what that day was to me and why I was on the trip. And they were great about it. They said, "You need a drink" and "We're going to have a good night." That was helpful, no doubt. But I also needed that moment by the water.

Eventually, we landed in Belgium. I went to the Swarovski Museum and bought a ring. It's kind of swirly with pink Swarovski crystals. It did not look like an engagement ring or a wedding band. It felt right.

Then onto Amsterdam, which, to this day, is one of my favorite places in the world. And not for the, wink, wink, obvious reasons. We stayed at a hostel (being the end of the trip, we'd finally graduated out of cabins). And I knew I'd be going home in a couple of days, so maybe I was more relaxed. We toured the Heineken factory and rode the canals. The last night, we all ate at a lively restaurant with amazing Asian food. I felt safe walking around at night. Something about the city made me feel cool. I fell in love with it.

Incidentally, I've been back to Holland probably five times. A friend's daughter got the lead role in a Dutch film called *EEP*, and I went to visit her and attend a screening. Another friend attended school in Utrecht for a few years, so I visited him. I also flew over with a business partner for a conference in Rotterdam. Every time I go, I fall more in love with the country. I finally had the chance to take Allan in 2022. And in the fall of 2024, I emceed the live portion of an industry conference. It's hard to explain, but I've always been drawn to Holland. And I was introduced to it that summer.

After Amsterdam, I had to figure out how to get home with four extra bags balanced on top of my traveler backpack—all of that in addition to the box I'd already shipped home from Munich. Cut to me on a rush-hour train in London, sweating and unable to move. When I got back to my grandmother's, we sat, and I told her all about the trip. I was exhausted but full of confidence. I felt ready to go home, face my circumstances, and rebuild my life. If I could spend thirty days on a bus with thirty other people and sleep in cabins all across Europe, I figured I could do anything.

Joking aside, I truly had faced my limits—a number of times, in every place we visited and all our excursions. Whitewater rafting was totally outside my comfort zone, but I did it. I felt incredibly anxious on Jungfrau mountain. But I made it to the top and stayed up there. There are endless examples from the trip, times when I learned I can do more than I thought I could.

And I learned from people who live in different parts of the world, saw how they understand life, soaked up their points of views. I can't believe I called my dad on the third day saying I wanted to come home. Instead, I came out the other side feeling better about myself, more confident in my abilities, and more comfortable pushing against my edges.

To be clear, that doesn't mean every limit is worth expanding. We went trout fishing in Austria. There were a ton of fish, but I couldn't catch one to save my life. I quit within an hour. Fishing is not my jam (and neither is real estate, but we'll get to that later). And that's fine. It doesn't have to become my job. It's not a limit I need to expand. But I tried it. That's the whole point. On the other hand, I learned I'm good at negotiating. Today, in my job, I negotiate all the time: with clients, vendors, and partners. Sometimes I even read and negotiate my own contracts, rather than using a lawyer (but that is not a professional recommendation).

My point is that it's important to try everything since that's how you figure out what you like and don't like, what you're good at and not good at. That way, you can better navigate life's path. There are possibilities in life you don't even know are out there yet. When you know what you do and don't like and what your skillsets are, you're less likely to pass up opportunities and more likely to say no to bad fits without second-guessing your decision. For example, I have determined over time that I don't do keynote speeches. I'm very vocal about this. I don't like them. They're not my thing.

When I first had that response, I asked myself if I was just being scared, if I was putting a limit on myself out of fear. So I went through a little process of asking myself questions over and over for a couple of months. I came out the other end having determined that I'm not a PowerPoint presenter. I wasn't just saying that as an excuse because I am terrified of public speaking. I don't like PowerPoint.

I don't like making them. I think they're boring as hell. They're good for some people but not for me. Sure, I could do a keynote without a PowerPoint, but also I don't want to talk on my own for forty-five minutes. I prefer dialogue. Most importantly, learning that about myself is part of what helped me find my superpower to create safe spaces for interesting dialogue.

Nowadays, I decline keynote invitations all the time. I offer an alternative: to moderate a fireside chat or a panel. Ultimately, they just don't know yet that that's really what they want to pay me to do anyway. I also found that I could make my own version of a keynote; who dictates what a keynote must be or look like anyway? Mine offer an opportunity for a fireside chat at the beginning, or I'll share my story, depending on the setting and audience, and then ask the audience questions that they discuss in groups. This makes it interactive and keeps everyone engaged.

When you learn what you do and don't like, and are and aren't good at, you also learn about your boundaries. But again, it's important to question yourself in the moment to make sure you're not just setting a boundary out of fear.

While you're exploring, pay attention to what you find joy in. My discovery around negotiating wasn't just that I'm good at it but also that I think it's fun. As for learning from other people, you don't necessarily have to travel the world. For example, during the pandemic, I put together a global, virtual supply-chain happy hour every week. People gathered from all over the world: Australia, Panama, Canada. We helped each other through lockdowns, heartbreak, and challenging professional scenarios.

We shared advice on how to build businesses. We celebrated each others' wins and birthdays. We laughed. We cried. I miss it. Everyone has gone about their busy lives, and some have decided to go in different directions, and of course that's life. When we were all engaged, it was a special place to be and to look forward to every week.

Still, if you can travel, there's nothing else quite like it. Be careful, though, because there's a delicate balance between learning from other people and learning from yourself. Confidence also comes from independence. The Contiki tour was something I did on my own. I had to figure out a lot on that trip.

> **WHETHER YOU ENTER A ROOM WITH OTHER PEOPLE OR ALONE, IT'S STILL YOU WALKING THROUGH THAT DOOR.**

Even though I was surrounded by people, that trip was the essence of independence. Independence breeds confidence because we have to learn to be comfortable in our own standing in order even to walk into a room. Whether you enter a room with other people or alone, in a corporate role or just as a human being, it's still you walking through that door.

Independence is the core of confidence because it allows you to be OK to be yourself. Otherwise, we fall into codependency, taking on other people's tendencies and likes and dislikes. We lose ourselves. That's exactly what I had done with my fiancé. The more confident you are in yourself, the less likely you'll get absorbed into someone else's thoughts or perspective. What's right for them might not be right for you. So dedicate time to figure out what's right for you.

IF YOU DON'T UNDERSTAND YOURSELF, IT'S HARD TO GENERATE SELF-WORTH.

This is also how you'll understand and build up your value. To return to the keynote example, when I decline, that doesn't mean I don't have value to offer them. Rather, I changed the perspective around value by instead offering my panel-moderation skills. That's the value they want to pay for.

If you don't understand yourself, it's hard to generate self-worth. Because you'll be perpetually thinking about how others see you, how they respond to things you say, do, or decline. You'll live in regret without even really understanding why you feel regretful because you aren't certain whether or not opportunities you passed on were actually good for you. Or you'll feel guilty for letting someone down. Self-worth comes from understanding yourself, and that happens by expanding perspective and living life, saying yes to opportunities, and being OK when something doesn't feel right for you.

It all requires vulnerability: first, to even acknowledge that you need to expand your horizons. A lot of people decide they're good with whatever they've learned so far or that they are too old to change or learn new things. Other times, they close themselves off because they are afraid of saying or doing the wrong things. That's burying self-worth, not building it up.

Traveling and experiencing new cultures changes how we approach our lives. Sometimes you don't have to actually travel to be influenced by a different culture. My husband Allan's family is from Trinidad and have introduced me to Soca music. It's changed my life in so many positive ways. Singing and dancing have always been a positive part of my life. Certainly, I did my time on the dance floor during my rave era. And in high school I took singing lessons. My teacher was the crazy old lady in *Happy Gilmore* (you remember the scene: an air conditioner drops on her).

Singing has always been my solace in turmoil. I sing to feel better. I sing for fun. I have never shared it publicly. I don't do karaoke. But I sing constantly on my own and with my family. And no music makes me feel as happy as Soca. It's an offshoot of calypso and was developed in Trinidad in the 1970s. Soca literally means the soul of calypso.

It's upbeat and colorful. The first time I heard it, it made me smile, made me want to dance. The melodies make me happy. It just fills my soul. I haven't been to Trinidad or Tobago yet and would love to visit sometime soon. We play it at home, in the car. We blasted it from the speakers in our golf cart while we drove through the community, so now I guess I'm the one spreading it around.

***

That night in Venice, after seeing another couple get married in Saint Mark's Square on my wedding day, I was very vulnerable. And I'm glad I chose to tell some people on the bus what had happened and what I was going through. After I took some time to myself, they were able to help me and pull me back into the world.

The time I took to myself was just as important, though. If you feel like you have to be with people all the time just to get through your struggles, you're actually avoiding the work rather than healing. That night, my decision not to do what everybody else was doing felt like a real accomplishment. I could've buried my sadness and gone drinking and dancing—I mean, I did eventually go drinking and dancing—but I chose to sit with myself and my struggle for a minute first.

When I booked that trip, I didn't know how profoundly it would affect me. I only felt an urge to keep moving forward. I guess I knew I was running away from sadness, but I didn't know that run would deliver me to healing. Life is lived forward and understood backward.

CHAPTER 7

BOUNDARIES AREN'T WALLS BUT BLUEPRINTS

I GUESS THE MOMENT I REALIZED BONNIE WAS TAKING advantage of me was when she asked me to cut my honeymoon short so I could come back and work a trade show with her for free. I declined. She became upset and said I was leaving her in a bad spot—by not *cutting my honeymoon short to work for her for free*. That was the point when I saw what our relationship really was, that she was using me.

Another red flag from around that time: in a speech at my wedding, she said I like golden showers. To be clear, it was definitely a *joke*. But no shade if that's your thing. Anyway, I didn't even hear it when she said it, thank goodness. She said this in front of my friends and family, Allan's friends and family, my boss, and all the VPs and their families at my wedding. When someone told me a few months after the wedding, I felt so embarrassed that I had let this person give a toast.

Who says that about someone at their wedding? Was she trying to ruin one of the best days of my life? Was she jealous that not all the attention was on her so she had to cut me down to make herself feel better? When I confronted Bonnie, she told me I couldn't take a joke. It was gaslighting at its finest. It was the last time I set foot into her apartment. I left that day knowing our friendship was over.

I had started working with her years earlier. In my late twenties, I got the feeling, *Maybe, actually, my lifelong goal of taking over the family business is* not *my destiny*. (Turns out that was right, of course, though not for the reasons I anticipated.) I started to think maybe I didn't want to be in that particular business for the rest of my life. What else was there to do in the world besides supply chain? I needed to know. So, in addition to the work at my parents' company, I poured myself into helping somebody else build a company. It was fulfilling to help a female entrepreneur develop her business. But mostly I was motivated to explore what I was capable of.

Bonnie and I met on a sales call. She was building a makeup brand. I cold-called her and asked to set up a meeting to discuss her customs needs because she was bringing in products from New York. I ended up at her apartment that day, and we hit it off. We talked about customs as well as everything else in our lives. I signed her as a client. Then we went on a crazy five-year ride where we each did a lot for each other. She was my client and also asked favors of me, and I offered to help, the whole time picking up new skills. I felt wanted and appreciated at first, and that had been missing for a long time.

I should tell you that she's a classic narcissist, which also means she was fun. I spent a lot of time in my early life around narcissists, and I think that aspect of her personality was comfortably familiar. There was a lot of gaslighting, but that was also familiar to me from the years I was bullied. As messed up as it sounds, I was gaining from her a sense of belonging. I felt like I had friends.

Over time, I basically became her business manager—unpaid.

The relationship developed organically. Still, I could've set boundaries at some point. But I didn't. I was really good at the work I did. I was able to get her a makeup contract with one of the local football teams. She often put me onstage or in front of a camera. I don't discredit the valuable skills I learned from my time with her. But at the same time, she was getting free labor. She didn't even pay me for gas. I went to trade shows with her two or three times a week and never even got commission on what I sold.

I don't know what I was thinking.

I guess I was having fun. We were meeting all sorts of people. We went to Toronto International Film Festival parties. I got free makeup. And business was booming. Women lined up at trade shows to buy products. It all made me feel good, like I was a part of something. But I had completely erased all boundaries around my self-worth. I say *erased*, but honestly, I don't know that I'd ever had them before. Suffice it to say, I didn't value myself enough to have a conversation with her about getting paid.

It's one thing to work for free for a little while in order to get your foot in the door. But if you're going to do something for free, your next step is to turn that into something paid, not continue doing it for free. And because I worked for free, I gained no respect from her. I shouldn't have let it go for as long as I did.

Then it got to the point where I was lending her money for things. (I know, I know—that's how little self-worth I had at the time. And, as I realize now, one of my MOs back then was to buy friendships.) After a while, she stopped paying me back. Then there was the incredibly strange and disrespectful joke at my wedding and the expectation that I would cut my honeymoon short to work more for free. That was when I saw clearly what was happening. I saw how much I was doing for this company that I had no equity in and for which I received no salary. Armed with these new realizations, the first thing I did was—drumroll, please—blame myself.

Have you ever felt that your self-worth is tied to other people's actions or reactions? Even as I saw that I was being used, I thought to myself, *I could've done more* and *Maybe I should leave my honeymoon early because that's the right thing to do* and *I don't want to upset her* and, worst of all, *I don't want her to be mad at me*. I was still prioritizing her needs above my own. That's where I was mentally at that time in my life. I didn't put myself first. I didn't have boundaries. I was more concerned about losing a friend than getting what I needed. And, anyway, she was never really my friend!

FREE SERVES NO ONE.

It took a lot of time and therapy for me even to reach those realizations. Probably only in the last two or three years have I been able to understand and articulate what happened. I'm still learning, especially through my advocacy and networking, which have allowed me to develop my perspective around how women treat each other, how we value ourselves, how we don't ask for what we need financially or otherwise. Free serves no one. It only causes resentment within the person who one day realizes they're not being valued or appreciated.

Free only benefits the person making money off of the relationship. If we keep working for free as women, we will keep expecting women to work for free. I'd rather promote the fact that women need to get paid (and equally to their male counterparts). Otherwise, we're showing the next generation that it's OK for them to devalue themselves too and training society to believe that women don't deserve payment for some of the work they do. We don't talk about it enough. Changing our individual mindsets around it will eventually change the collective mindset.

When women expect each other to do things for free, that teaches us and the market not to invest in each other or in the work we do. When I was building my business, I did some things for free to build up credibility—but in retrospect I see that I also did them because the market expected me to work for free. I also agreed to a handful of in-kind partnerships, wherein two organizations basically do each other a favor, tit for tat. But they always ended up lopsided, where I gave more than I got. So I don't do those anymore—in part because, as I mentioned earlier, 95 percent of my team are women-owned businesses, and I don't want to set a bad example.

* * *

My relationship with Bonnie blew up after I got back from my honeymoon. I finally decided to assert boundaries. It did not go well.

We met for lunch. I wasn't sure how she would respond, so I wanted to be in a public place. My anxiety was through the roof. I was shaking when I walked into the restaurant. But I thought, *I need to stand up for myself*. It had been a long time coming.

I told her our relationship wasn't working, that I couldn't do everything I was doing for free anymore. I pointed out that I was with her two or three times a week. I said that when she expected me to be at a trade show with her instead of on my honeymoon, it revealed that she lacked respect for me. I told her I felt disrespected, I was having a hard time getting over it, and that if we were going to try to get through this and continue working together, I would need equity and to start getting paid for my time, including back wages.

A classic narcissist does not like to be confronted with their own misgivings. She berated me for an hour. She felt like I was betraying her. (When you don't set boundaries at the beginning and then try to assert them later, that often happens.) I don't remember exactly what she said. I've blocked it from my memory. It was nasty. When I walked out of the restaurant, I felt like I had just crawled out of a washing machine. I cried the whole way home, not quite understanding what had just happened or which way was up.

After that, we had a phone call, throughout which she berated me more. At that point, I knew there was no coming back. The trust was gone. There had never been respect. She was treating me so badly. And she still owed me money! Even if you don't take into account back wages, I had loaned her quite a bit by this point. It was clear she simply didn't value me or my time. The whole relationship had been based on what I could do for her. I don't know if she even liked me as a person. Clearly, she wasn't thinking of my needs, only her own.

If you're in a situation without boundaries and you sense that you're giving more than you should and aren't being valued, that's your first clue to either set boundaries or leave. Other clues: if the work you're doing for free is costing you relationships because it's taking you away from your loved ones. Or if you're investing actual money in addition to not being paid. Or even if it just doesn't feel good anymore—that's enough of a red flag on its own.

SOMETIMES HOW WE FEEL ABOUT OURSELVES LEADS US TO PLAY IT SMALL.

When I was with Bonnie, I felt small. She was dynamic, popular, beautiful. I admired her and felt that I didn't measure up. Sometimes how we feel about ourselves leads us to play it small, to stay within the realm of what we're comfortable with. For example, we don't go for that promotion because we see we don't have 100 percent of the qualifications, whereas other people (especially guys) would go for the job even if they only had 60 percent. When we're in our feelings and, especially if we're not feeling good about ourselves, we end up playing small, when there's so much more we could do with our lives, so much more impact to make in the world.

There's a price for playing it small. I was no longer willing to pay it. I was finally standing up. I did the next best thing for myself. I took Bonnie to court.

At the time, this felt like a huge step. Now that I'm an entrepreneur, I understand that if you're going to be in business, you'll sometimes have to go to court. It's uncomfortable, but it's the way of life for entrepreneurs. In this case, it was small-claims court. I don't even remember how much I sued her for. I think it was $5,000?

When she was served the papers, she got extremely pissed off. I received a bunch of nasty text messages. My anxiety went through the roof. Then, the day we appeared in court, the judge was basically like, *I don't wanna hear it—you guys need to go into the hallway and fix this.*

Standing in the hallway, she berated me again. *You are so freaking crazy* and *I can't even believe we're here* and *You did all of this*. It was awful. I fired up every nerve and neuron in my body just to keep my cool and not start crying. But ultimately, there was nothing she could do. She had borrowed the money. She knew she owed it to me. She never made any plan to pay it back while she meanwhile went on vacations. She was an adult who had made choices, and now she had to deal with them. We ended up coming to terms: she would pay me $2,800, given to me in postdated checks. And then I was done with her.

But it took years for me to recover. Her treatment of me triggered all of my trauma. It made me feel I wasn't good enough. It brought back all of the bullying, second-guessing, questioning whether I was a bad friend, and worrying what she might say about me to other people. All of that said, there *were* elements of that relationship that have helped me later in life, that led me to where I am today, including certain skillsets, yes, but also this: part of my advocacy work is to try to keep people from ending up in similar situations.

What is the one thing that makes you question your value? My personal answer to that question would be that I often feel I'm not doing enough. That's embarrassing to admit. For example, two days ago, one of my assistants, Emily, sent me a Slack message saying, "You've won four awards since the beginning of the year." At that exact moment, I had been sitting on the couch thinking, *I don't do enough.* Then her message popped in, I realized that obviously I was doing enough, and therefore, I suddenly had a very different strong feeling—but still along the lines of *What is wrong with me?*

What causes me to think I don't do enough? Comparison. Scrolling on social media through people's accolades and beautiful photos. I get caught in negative cycles of thinking, especially whenever I'm comparing myself to others. It ties directly into self-worth. It leads me to question my value. The internal dialogue in such moments is kind of embarrassing. I have to remind myself that I actually do a lot and accomplish a lot in a year.

> **I'LL ADMIT IT HERE: THERE ARE DAYS WHEN I THINK I DON'T DO ENOUGH, AND THEN I HAVE TO FIND THE STRENGTH TO TELL MYSELF THE TRUTH AND EXIT THAT MINDSET.**

I don't tell people that I sit on the couch some days and think, *Everyone else is so much better off than I am.* But the truth is that everyone feels that way, even if nobody talks about it. Do you? So I'll admit it here: there are days when I think I don't do enough, and then I have to find the strength to tell myself the truth and exit that mindset.

The moment Emily's Slack message interrupted my cycle of compare and despair, I felt better because I saw evidence that actually I was doing enough. The evidence was undeniable, which led to the perspective shift I needed. Maybe that "I'm not doing enough" feeling is really about pressure to keep up. Nothing ever feels like enough. That's the pressure of society.

But I do think it's linked to self-worth. If you truly believed in the value of what you were doing—in the energy you were putting into your work—you would feel like it was enough. You'd recognize your own value and worth. And that's all part of why it's so important to value your worth financially.

> **A LACK OF BOUNDARIES SHOWCASES TO OTHER PEOPLE HOW YOU FEEL ABOUT YOURSELF. THAT CAN GIVE THEM PERMISSION TO EXPLOIT YOU.**

Working for free devalues not just yourself but all women. Perhaps that's why women often feel like we're never doing enough—because we're expected to keep doing more. But you don't have to take it all on. You can maintain balance by learning to say no.

A lack of boundaries showcases to other people how you feel about yourself. That can give them permission to exploit you. When you have boundaries, on the other hand, you create a blueprint. That blueprint exists for yourself, allowing you to return to it whenever you want to be reminded of the reasons you created it. And it exists in order to show other people how to value you.

CHAPTER 8

PROGRESS OVER PERFECTION

IN THE EARLY 2010S, ALLAN AND I WERE LIVING IN A TOWNhouse and decided to get it painted. The painter asked if we wanted him to paint behind the builder mirror in the bathroom—you know those flat mirrors that are glued onto the wall. He said they're a pain to remove and I'd have to replace the drywall behind it. I said that Allan and I can't even hang a picture, so we definitely wouldn't be drywalling, and to please just paint around it. But after the walls were freshly done, that basic builder mirror looked even uglier.

I couldn't leave it like that, so I started researching ways to make a builder mirror prettier. But if we couldn't even hang a picture, how the hell were we supposed to DIY a frame. There had to be an easier way. So I invented one. I designed a frame kit for builder mirrors, comprised of separate pieces that you click together, depending on the size of your mirror. I ended up getting a patent for it. I haven't taken it to market (yet), but I own the patent. It's called Just Frame It, as in just frame that ugly builder mirror. I have a logo and everything.

During my last years at my parents' company, I actually pursued several side hustles (and, as I mentioned earlier, acquired a license to sell life insurance). It started simply because I've always been that way, been a learner and a doer. For example, during my first few years at my parents' company, and in part because I had skipped university, I looked for other ways to further my education. That ended up being correspondence classes. I took a purchasing course and one on international trade. I did seminars on real estate and one on investing. They were all building skills related to the business I was pursuing and planned one day to take over.

This was before online school, of course, so the school mailed me books. (Initially, I did these classes in night school, but I didn't feel comfortable walking through the parking lot at night, so I petitioned the school to let me do it by correspondence.) When I took a test, one of my bosses at work had to be a proctor, oversee me, and report back that I hadn't cheated. Eventually, my further education switched from classes and seminars to side hustles.

Again, my side hustles mostly supported my future plans to run the company. But in retrospect, and as I mentioned earlier, I think some part of me had also started to wonder if I should do something different with my career. But since I had only ever worked at one company, and it was the same one that had dominated my childhood and teen years as well, I didn't have a wide range of skillsets. In order to build them, I had to get creative. So I started throwing stuff against the wall. By *stuff*, I mean businesses.

I launched a technology company. And also a sweat-resistant makeup line for athletes, which somehow morphed into an Amazon-style distribution company. Then, believe it or not, some business partners of mine ended up getting the rights to Bonnie's company, which we turned into a monthly subscription box. I had another side hustle handling the shipping for a shoe-wipe company. I started a rent-to-own real estate company. And a furniture-package company in Costa Rica. This was all happening in my late twenties and through my thirties. I wasn't getting rich off of any of them, but at least they were mine.

I realize I just wrote a chapter about the importance of not working for free, so I want to draw out a distinction. With *Let's Talk Supply Chain,* I didn't pay myself for the first three years, but the *company* was making money. I charged people for the business's services. I just wasn't pulling a salary from it. The same thing was happening with my various side hustles. As an entrepreneur, you will potentially have to work without a paycheck for some time. That doesn't mean you're not *charging* for the work you do.

My first company was a rent-to-own situation that ended up in disaster because of some stupid misunderstanding. Then, my brother and I explored a furniture package company in Costa Rica. He and I also flirted with buying a British food import company, but that fell through. And on and off for years, I dabbled in real estate. I told you earlier that it was not my jam. That conclusion isn't coming from me but from the universe.

I am not destined to be a landlord. I have had multiple rental properties and terrible experiences with each. I owned a house for a year and rented it out; the air conditioner was stolen twice, and the last tenant caused ten thousand dollars in damage. In another property I rented out, the tenant damaged it so much after one year that the carpets had to be replaced, and it took two cleaners four hours to clean 950 square feet.

My first company with actual legs was Shipz.com. I had always wanted to be in technology. My background was in freight forwarding and logistics. So I found business partners, and we created a platform that paired shippers with freight forwarders. When a company needed to ship products or raw materials, they'd work with a freight company to move those goods. We wanted to make it easier for both the shipper to find the company and for the freight company to find the right clients.

While we were building out the technology, we sought funding. After four years, we got an opportunity. But the terms were bad. And, at the time, one of my business partners had a heart attack and bypass surgery. Also, *Let's Talk Supply Chain* was blowing up. So instead of accepting the funding, I made the decision to sell Shipz.com. Although the technology wasn't quite there yet, we had built a strong brand and customer list. The buyers never ended up doing anything with it.

Before that endeavor, I knew nothing about building technology or about investment. I'd never had to go out and ask for money before. And then cut to me pitching investors left and right. I won a woman-in-tech award before I had even built anything, just because I had done a good job with the branding. That felt great.

I also learned some harder lessons. I do regret going into business with one of my partners. He didn't know as much about technology as he had said he did, and that was a costly learning experience. But I probably wouldn't have done anything differently because I didn't know what I was doing and sometimes you just have to jump in. That's part of the journey.

Everybody's going to make mistakes. To have a side hustle or build a business, you have to learn through mistakes. It's one of the straightest paths to growth. Of course, research what you can; talk to people and try to avoid whatever mistakes they made. That's another path to learning. But that can only help you so much.

For example, I had the opportunity to speak with one of the co-founders of Expedia to get his advice about what I was building. Honestly, it didn't help me. I still had my own mistakes to make. So don't let potential regrets stop you from jumping in. In fact, that's one of the purposes of starting a side hustle to begin with: to give yourself opportunities to make mistakes, to learn what you're capable of, and try new things.

If I'm being honest, one of the biggest lessons I learned from Shipz.com is that I'll never go down that road again. I learned how incredibly hard it is for women to get investment in general and especially in technology. More to the point, that kind of technology wasn't really for me. But at the time I thought I wanted it. I thought, *I want my own technology company, and we're going to hit it big, and everyone will love my idea. Who wouldn't want to invest in it?* Almost everybody, turns out. Today, I try to support women who are out there looking for investment for their companies because it's a dark road.

Before I sold the company, I had a phone call with a good friend of mine who owns his own technology company and had been mentoring me a bit. He said, "Why are you still doing Shipz? *Let's Talk Supply Chain* is taking off. It's working. And Shipz just pulls you down."

He was right. I was getting all this energy from recording and doing the podcast, and then Shipz sucked it all out of me. He helped me see that I needed to focus on what was naturally made for me, and that was the podcast.

That phone conversation happened the same week we received the lackluster investment offer, my business partner had a heart attack, and I won the woman-in-tech award. I just remember thinking, *Why is this so hard? Do I really want do it anymore?* I decided I didn't.

You'll almost always come to that point with a side hustle. That's the nature of a side hustle. Either it becomes your main thing, or you stop doing it. I was torn about selling Shipz, of course. I had spent so much time, energy, and resources on it. And I still knew that it could be a good thing.

But I just couldn't do it anymore. My friend was right: it was draining me of my superpower while there was something else feeding it. Although I had been feeling this myself for some time, I figured no one else noticed. When he said it out loud, I realized the decision was obvious.

Even though selling Shipz was the right choice in the long run, I was totally disappointed at the time. But I focused on all the things I've gained from the experience, the learning and growth. For example, I can converse knowledgeably with podcast guests from technology companies. A different kind of knowledge I gained was that I *didn't want* to work in technology. That's also important information for an entrepreneur. It helps you figure out not only which sectors to pursue but within those areas, what you'll want to cover yourself and what you'll want to outsource.

Knowing that technology isn't my jam made it easy for me to know which roles to hire first for the podcast. It requires quite a bit of social media. I'm not great at it, and I don't particularly enjoy it. So my first hire was a social-media expert. Then I brought on someone to do the graphics, another area in which I don't excel. I'm really good at B2B marketing but not B2C. Honestly, I think one of the reasons my other company failed is because I don't understand selling to consumers, yet I was doing all of that myself.

That brings me to the next company I started, a sweat-resistant makeup line for athletes called Sarah, Caroline, and Co. This was a passion project. I had learned a lot about the industry after working (for free) for Bonnie. And I've always worn makeup when playing sports. So I knew there were a few offering a makeup line of such products in the marketplace, and I knew exactly the kind of products the market lacked.

I quickly learned there was hardly a marketplace at all for female athletes. There was nowhere they could go to find all of the products and aids a female sports player wants and needs, like Epsom salts or specific balms. I envisioned turning Sarah, Caroline, and Co. into that marketplace. I contacted smaller companies who were making or selling products for female athletes and got their merchandise on my website.

It was an excellent idea. But I didn't have enough money for marketing and, as I said, didn't really understand consumer selling, unfortunately. There were other mistakes. I found a supplier in Korea that sold a liquid vitamin E I liked and ordered a whole pallet. I shouldn't have. We never found the customers, and I ended up donating most of our stock.

But there were so many wins along the way. I got my branding on the liquid vitamin E, as well as on face sheet masks I'd ordered, and the makeup from a supplier in New York. I remember my first photo shoot with the product, everything totally homegrown. It all looked great. That was a proud moment. And I figured out the Amazon distribution–type model. I built my own contracts. I was really proud of myself for building the website, ecosystem, and marketplace. All of the suppliers and vendors loved the idea and believed in it. We just never found the customers. Perhaps I was ahead of my time, and something like that would do well today.

I tried influencer marketing. I paid a high-end marketing company for a campaign. None of it resulted in sales. I was just pouring money into it but kept meeting brick walls. Then the pandemic hit, and I had to make a decision. In the end, I lost all the money I had put into inventory, pulled the product from the warehouse, donated some of it, and shipped the rest to a friend in Michigan. Then I tore down the website.

NO ONE IS KEEPING SCORE OF YOUR SUPPOSED WINS AND LOSSES.

It was sad, but it was all learning experiences. I don't think of things like that as failures. Once something doesn't work out, it doesn't mean you're a bad person or can't do hard things. It just means that it wasn't right. I think we should take the word *failure* out of our vocabulary. When things go south, just take a look at what you learned from the experience and carry it all with you into the next. For example, I learned you can have too many cooks in the kitchen when it comes to a pitch deck. I learned not to invest too much money in products until you have customers. And that if you're going to have a partner, you should vet them first to make sure they're cut out for entrepreneurship. And that you don't need a board of advisors with equity straight out of the gate. There was so much to carry with me.

Either way, no one is keeping score of your supposed wins and losses. When I shut down Sarah, Caroline, and Co. and sold Shipz, nobody cared. Nobody remembers. I didn't put out a statement on social media. They just quietly faded away. They're part of my journey and my story. I'm proud of myself for what I accomplished. And I value what I learned and was able to take to new experiences later.

Losing those companies didn't stop me from being an entrepreneur or moving forward with other projects. People get rocked by quote-unquote failure. And listen, if that's you, that's OK too—sometimes you have to go through the valley of death in order to come out the other side. But ultimately, it's all about how you respond to walking that path. It certainly shouldn't stop you from trying again. Fall apart if you need to, but then put yourself back together. There's no alternative to making mistakes, even if you play it safe. Don't let your fear of mistakes keep you from reaping the opportunities they provide, specifically, to pick up new skills and learn what you really want to do with your life.

That's how it worked for me, at least. It was because of my side hustles that I realized *Let's Talk Supply Chain* was where I really wanted to be. Like I said, it all came to a head during the pandemic. I felt spread thin and burned out. And I realized that people really wanted the podcast, it was making a difference, and I could earn actual money doing it.

Most importantly, I realized it was my favorite of all my projects. I'm able to create a safe space for conversation. That's what people were digging. The messages I received—"I love your show," "I listen to it all the time," "You make supply chain fun"—encouraged me as well. Some thinker once said, "You've got to try nine things before the tenth works out." *Let's Talk Supply Chain* wasn't my tenth, but it was the last one standing after ten, and the one I chose.

Even though I found my one thing, I'm still creating new projects within it. I launched the *Blended* podcast and Blended

Pledge. I created the Secret Society of Supply Chain, which is our membership group. And, frankly, if the membership group doesn't grow more before the end of the year, I'm going to pull the plug. It has not been a walk in the park. So you have to continue growing but also continue paring back. That's why, actually, I created three membership groups: ultimately, I'll keep one and drop the other two.

And the two that go away? That's not because they're failures. They're just irons I threw in the fire that never got used. Sometimes my podcast guests are uncomfortable talking about the mistakes they've made along the way. They're worried what other people will think of them. They've connected these supposed failures to their self-worth.

MAKE MISTAKES PART OF YOUR STORY.

But when I have guests who do talk about their mistakes, the audience eats it up. Those end up being our most popular episodes. We all struggle with this. We should talk about it more. You can't walk through life without mistakes. Why hide from them? Make them part of your story.

I used to think I needed confidence to try something new. At first, the lack of confidence paralyzed me. But I soon realized, through my journey with side hustles, that I could just try something and the confidence would come later. Or maybe it wouldn't—and that's ok too. I realized that confidence itself was a kind of perfection getting in the way of my progress. Forget confidence; just start. As long as you're always getting better, even if you sometimes take a few steps back, there's not much more anyone can ask of you.

CHAPTER 9

I BURIED HER IN A FRENCH PRESS

AT THE BEGINNING OF THE PANDEMIC, BEFORE THE LOCKdowns, I decided I would fly to England and stay with Lesley so she wouldn't be alone. Unfortunately, I didn't make the decision quick enough. Lockdown happened, and all I could do was check in over the phone and coordinate with her neighbors to check in too. Lesley was my grandmother. Well, she was my stepgrandmother. We were very close. She had always been in my life. I grew up spending summers with my grandfather and her in the UK.

During the pandemic, Lesley was admitted to a hospital and never came back out. One day, her best friend found her in a mess (let's just put it that way) and put her in an ambulance. Turns out her kidneys had been failing for years. She'd refused to see a doctor. The day she went to the hospital was the day I found out about her illness. I didn't know how bad it was at first. Her family in England knew more than I did, but they didn't share much, which was frustrating. By that time, Lesley's health was irreparable.

My cousin called me over WhatsApp, and the second he told me she was in the hospital, I sat down on the living room floor and started crying. I just knew. In that moment, I knew she would never come out. And I knew she was all alone, since no one was allowed in hospitals during the pandemic.

I had sensed that something was wrong four years prior. She and I had been on a road trip. I drove her around the UK to see family members and attend a wedding. We stayed in a hotel together, and she kept getting up in the middle of the night for strange reasons—to make sure her purse was still there or that the room was locked. I was terrified she'd leave the room and get lost, so I didn't sleep at all. She couldn't be still. And she couldn't remember things.

I told everyone in the family that something was wrong. Being in Canada, there was only so much I could do. Everyone else tried too. They did their best to get her to the doctor, but she just wouldn't go.

When my cousin called, he didn't have the details. But I knew, *This is the end.* I also knew in my heart that she wouldn't even last the five days I would be required to quarantine if I tried to fly to England. I pulled myself together enough to call her. She was frantic. She just wanted to be at home and kept saying, "I'm going home soon," and then asking anyone who would listen if she could go home soon. I tried my best to keep her calm and distract her with stories of the lockdown in Canada. It was so distressing. I hated to hear the anxiety and panic in her voice.

Lesley had always said she wanted to go at the same time as my grandfather. She outlived him by fifteen years, but they died at the same time of day, 2:00 a.m. Her autopsy confirmed she had both kidney disease and Alzheimer's.

The family started making arrangements immediately. She was cremated. And the funeral would be three or four weeks later. I couldn't attend because of the pandemic. But I made plans to get out there in August. And I asked her niece, who was the executor, not to clean out her house until I could get there to help her. I had a lot of stuff there, and I also wanted some keepsakes.

I wrote and recorded something about what she had meant to me and how much I loved her. "Our parents give us life," I said. "Our grandparents give us a sense of who we are and where we came from." I told some fun stories of things we'd done together, including that last road trip around the UK. I tried to explain what she had given me that so few others have: "She was so proud of me. Everyone in Shepperton High Street knew my name and knew that I was Lesley's granddaughter. She would tell the ladies at the Princess Alice shop how long I was in town and how much she would miss me when I left."

My family played the video during the ceremony, which I attended over the Internet, and that made me feel part of it. Still, I was so frustrated and upset that I couldn't be part of the plans, especially because the funeral wasn't like Lesley at all. During the service, I was crying in grief and also screaming at the screen. It was a tough day.

The family planned to gather again for a burial service in August, when I would be in town. I was put in charge of arrangements and was happy for the opportunity to be in England and plan something I felt Lesley would have wanted. I contacted a cemetery and bought a plot and a headstone. A week before I arrived, her niece had a dumpster delivered to Lesley's house, ripped the place apart, and put everything in the garbage. I was gutted. Lesley's best friend saw it happening and went dumpster diving that night to grab things for me, pictures and heirlooms.

This woman was in her eighties, picking stuff out of a dumpster. To be fair, Lesley's niece had saved a few things for me, whatever she thought I might have wanted, including photos of my grandfather, which I appreciated. But she threw out mementos from the curio cabinet, crystal Lesley had collected over the years, and my personal possessions that had been in the home. It all ended up in the garbage.

I quarantined for five days at a friend's house. I had to mail in negative Covid tests that week as proof. Then, I headed up to Leicestershire to stay with my cousins. We had a day or two together, before we drove in two cars to Sunbury for the burial. I was in a car with my female cousins. We stopped for Starbucks on the way, and I couldn't hold it together.

I kept asking, "How can I get through today with the whole family counting on me if I can't keep it together?" My cousins held my hands and said they were there for me no matter what and that crying was OK. During my grandfather's funeral fifteen years earlier, I was told that I had to be strong for the family and couldn't cry, so it was such a relief to hear something different this time. Then we all went to the house.

Suffice it to say that when I got to Lesley's home, it no longer felt like I was walking into my childhood home away from home. Everything had been wiped away. I wanted to buy the place, to keep it in the family, but I didn't have enough money or time. I knew this would be my last visit. And there wasn't much time. I walked through the house, full of memories. I visited the spot in the backyard, where some of my grandfather's ashes are buried. I found the box of items her niece had left me and threw it in the car.

We walked into the kitchen. There on the counter was an urn containing the rest of my grandfather's ashes and, next to it, a white box. I thought, *No way, this can't be.* When I opened the white box, there were her ashes in a plastic bag.

Holy shit, I thought, *What am I going to do? No one had told me there wasn't an urn. Isn't that kind of what you do—bury ashes in an urn?* They literally dumped her in a plastic bag and put her in a box. All of the preparations I had made, while coordinating the burial, and no one told me there was no urn?! It felt disrespectful to bury her in a plastic bag in a box. I had a pit in my stomach about it. I knew I would regret it for the rest of my life.

I had already missed her funeral. I wanted to do right by her, to honor her. I had to figure out how to bury her ashes in a respectful manner. Another cousin was there with me. I asked her, "What are we going to do?"

"There's a garden shop close by," she said. "I bet we can grab something from there." But there was no time. We had twenty minutes, and it takes ten just to get to the cemetery.

I don't know what came over me, but I started opening cupboards frantically. I don't know why; the house had been gutted. But I just had this instinct to check the cupboards. Sure enough, there was one over by the microwave that was chock full. The family had missed it somehow, when they emptied the house. There were glasses and jugs in there. And among it all was a box that had never been opened, containing a French press, with a receipt in it from 1992.

I grabbed a red jug and the boxed French press and asked, "Which are we burying her in?"

"Oh my God," my cousin said, and we both started laughing. Then her daughter went into another room because she couldn't even handle being a part of whatever was happening, and honestly, I wasn't sure I could either, but here we were. We chose the French press.

My whole intention was to be reverent about the burial process. And suddenly I was scooping her ashes into a French press from 1992. It was ridiculous.

First, I spooned out some of the ashes to keep separately because I planned to have them turned into a charm for a necklace (which I had made in the UK since you can't fly with human remains). And then we just started transferring the rest. We had to pour half of it into my grandfather's urn because the French press wouldn't hold all of it, and there was extra room with my grandfather. To fit the rest in the press, we had to remove the middle part, the actual press and metal rod. That meant there was a little hole at the top of the container. But what else could we do?

My cousin was watching me with some amount of horror. I

just kept saying, "I'm not burying her in a plastic bag in a box." We had to do what we had to do.

Still, the whole time we were laughing and crying because it was just so stupid. I couldn't believe I was going to bury my grandmother in a French press. But for some reason, that choice *didn't* feel disrespectful. It's hard to explain, but that whole day, I felt as if I was being guided by something. I trusted and followed each instinct. I was thinking about both the emotional and practical aspects of the day. Only later did I wonder what the hell the rest of the family would think. Regardless, I knew that Lesley would have thought it all hilarious.

She was just fun that way. And not traditional. She was five-foot-two, with a posh English accent. Everyone knew when she was coming because you'd hear the click click of her high heels. Walking down the street, she talked to everyone. She was very quirky. And she loved to laugh. I just knew she'd be OK with what we were doing.

I also knew she would love to have some of her ashes mixed with my grandfather's. They were two peas in a pod, always dancing and laughing. Now they could dance together forever. On her gravestone, I had already chosen the words, "Together, they dance again." As for the French press, she did love to drink coffee. I didn't realize it at the moment, but in the grand scheme of things, the French press made perfect sense. She and I were always going out for coffee. We'd visit the charity stops and then stop for coffee, or go to Kingston and stop for coffee, or I would visit and sit on her couch over coffees while she smoked a cigarette. That French press tied together a lot of memories. It felt like I was supposed to find it that day.

We left the house and arrived at the cemetery on time. It had been raining but stopped the moment we drove up. The sun came out. I think that was Granddad and Lesley watching over us. Others in my family were there, along with some of her friends. I walked over to where my great uncle was sitting by the plot.

"I haven't told anybody yet, and I don't know if we should," I said to him, "but I had to pour her ashes into a French press."

His eyes grew large.

I said, "You cannot make a face. They're all watching us. I'll tell you the story later." I took the press out of the bag enough to show only him. His eyes silently said, *Oh. My. God.*

Then it was time. I placed Lesley, Granddad, and the press in the ground, and dropped some papers and pictures in there. No one noticed the press. There was a small ceremony. I said a few words and broke down crying. My cousin spoke and cried. My great uncle told lovely stories. We poured some dirt into the plot. We got in our cars to head to the pub we had rented out for food and drinks. Two seconds after we got in our cars, it started dumping rain again, after having just been bright and sunny. Like I said, the whole day felt guided, curated.

At the pub, I came clean about the French press. I wasn't sure how everyone would take it. But by that point, I had decided the decision was fitting and funny, and I hoped they would agree. I also hoped the situation could provide some levity to a day filled with grief. So I just came out with it, saying somewhat coyly, "Guys, we buried her in a French press."

They all thought about it for a minute and decided it made total sense because Lesley loved coffee. Her best friend told me she thought Lesley would adore the idea of being buried in a French press. Now, whenever we visit the gravesite, we take coffee. We say we're going to have coffee with Lesley and Grandad. We sit and have a coffee together.

Years later, I can't stop thinking about the fact that one cupboard had been left untouched. And that the French press itself had been untouched—for twenty-nine years. But I also think about my instincts. Thank God, I wasn't second-guessing myself that day. Something told me not to accept the plastic bag in the box and to start searching, even though we were late, and even though the house had been emptied. I could've fallen apart in that moment. I could have blamed her niece for emptying the house. I could have victimized myself (definitely something I've done before). Instead, I followed my instincts and started opening doors.

OUR GUTS CAN USUALLY GUIDE US, IF WE LET THEM.

I haven't always trusted my instincts. Sometimes I've talked myself out of my instincts and ended up hiring the wrong people or befriending the wrong people. Even today, I still sometimes forget to trust my instincts. But whenever I do remember to listen to my gut, situations tend to work out. Our guts can usually guide us, if we let them.

Listening to mine has also helped me a lot in therapy. I've always had a heightened sense of awareness, more than most people. Sometimes, when I'm telling stories in therapy, I'll catch myself in the middle and realize that it's actually the "same" story: of a time I didn't listen to my gut and ended up in trouble. Seeing the pattern helps me break it.

And then, when I have an experience like searching Lesley's house, finding a French press, burying her in it, and having those decisions lead to a beautiful family tradition of having coffee at her gravesite, I'm reminded of the incredible benefits of trusting your gut and of the healing it can lead to.

IF YOU TURN SOMEONE INTO THE BAD GUY, THEN YOU DON'T HAVE TO FACE YOUR PART IN WHAT HAPPENED.

Usually, the times I'm able to listen to my instincts occur when I don't have an opportunity to think too much about a decision. On the other hand, I can't hear my instincts whenever I get too focused on the wrong thing, my head space is negative, I'm obsessing over something that happened and what I could have done differently, or obsessing over why certain things happen to me. Overthinking gets in your way. I try not to let myself do it—not least because that kind of rumination leads to storytelling, and I don't always have the story right! I'll remember things differently or insert details based on prior trauma or current doubts. Several times in my life, I have done this in such a way that I turned someone else into a bad guy and convinced myself they were intentionally trying to hurt me. It can be a defense mechanism: if you turn them into the bad guy, then you don't have to face your part in what happened. Only later did I realize the stories were fiction.

Now, when making decisions, I try to shut out the overthinking part of my brain and tap into a different kind of awareness. That awareness, whether guided by myself or whatever caused the sun to break through the clouds during Lesley's ceremony, has led not only to some beautiful moments in life but to a deeper relationship with and love for myself.

I think about the various versions of me I have been throughout my life. I've kept some with me and said goodbye to others. And that makes me think of the French press. I buried Lesley in it, but of course she's still with me—quite literally, as I had my grandfather's and Lesley's ashes made into a pendant that I wear around my neck. It's similar to what happens to past versions of myself.

As I grow and change, I'm always necessarily leaving parts of myself behind. In some ways, these parts of me are dead, but what I learned from them and the compassion I have for them live on and will always be a part of me. When you grow and change, it's kind of like burying a body but keeping the spirit. You don't need a formal casket—just grab something from the cabinet. Put whatever you're leaving behind in a French press and then say yes to that night out.

CHAPTER 10

LABELS DON'T DEFINE YOUR IDENTITY; YOU DO

I WAS SITTING ON A PLANE WITH THE CEO OF A LOGISTICS company, who told me his company had just been bought. Later, he mentioned that he never says yes to speaking engagements because he already gets plenty of attention.

I interjected, "OK, but what are you going to do once your contract ends?"

When a company is bought, its CEO generally stays on for a certain period of contracted time and then leaves. He said, "I'm going to move into consulting."

"So what happens when the invitations to speak and the likes on your LinkedIn posts dry up?" I asked. "You'll no longer be a CEO of a big-name company that people recognize. So how will you get gigs?"

He'd never thought of it that way before. He realized that maybe he should have. I advised him to start saying yes to speaking engagements now and to start talking about his consulting plans now. That way he'd plant the seeds for his future and get everyone, including himself, accustomed to hearing him talk about something other than being the CEO of a logistics company.

I have conversations like that all the time. I spoke with a woman recently, who decided to leave her position without another job. She told me she was having a hard time because she was used to receiving a lot of attention and perks as a senior leader in a top-tier company, but now she no longer had access to that.

Sometimes when we make these decisions, we don't think through the ramifications. We only know what we know until we're in a new and different circumstance. She couldn't have imagined the impact that losing her job and title would have on her mental health. Now she was in a complete identity crisis because she was no longer going to have a title. She had attached her self-worth to it. Without it, who or what would she be?

I certainly experienced similar feelings when our family business closed its doors, and I went from being a director of sales and marketing to being out on my ass, when no one would hire me and taking a receptionist job at a tennis club where I mopped floors.

We do this not only in the workplace. We attach our self-worth and identity to all sorts of titles. A lot of women in society feel pressured to have children, for example. Perhaps you have wondered at some point, *Who am I if I don't have kids? Who am I in my community otherwise? Since our society thinks women should have children, will I be viewed as a failure if I don't?* I think this is especially hard on women who want to have children but can't. They're actually trying to do the thing that conforms to societal pressure and nevertheless feel rejected.

From a very young age, I was unsure about having children. It was never something I knew in my belly that I wanted to do. And anyway, I didn't think about it for a long time because I was rarely with anybody I would have considered having children with. So I suppressed that conversation for a long time. Then I met my husband, and now I have stepchildren. There's a whole *other* title. What does that one mean? I'm not really their mother.

We're not related by blood. But I'm certainly an influential figure in their lives.

Part of me has always wanted to adopt. There are so many kids out there born into unimaginable circumstances. At one point, I even wondered if it might be nice to have a biological child with my husband. But I didn't want to be pregnant or give birth. That's just who I am.

For a long time, I seriously considered surrogacy. But I couldn't stomach paying a hundred grand for it. Holy crackers, you need to seriously want a child to pay that bill. At one point, my husband and I tried. That lasted two weeks. I thought, *This is too much for me*. I didn't want to do it anymore. It was stressful. All of the pregnancy tests and then nothing was happening. It wasn't for me.

And yet. I totally went through the questioning. I asked myself, *If I don't have children, who am I in the community?* I even asked myself, *Who will take care of me when I am older?* That's a horrible reason to have kids, but I am only human, and I'm pretty sure I am not the only one who has thought this way. All of these thoughts made me feel defensive, but there's no one to blame. Possibly not even myself, since I might not even be physically capable of getting pregnant. I simply don't know. Honestly, part of what spurred me to try that one time was this horrible feeling in the back of my mind that kept asking, *Who will take care of me when I'm older?*

That is not the right reason to have children. Then again, it's always been one of the main reasons anyone has children. Still, it feels self-centered. That question was running through my mind the whole time. But then I also think about Lesley. She had no children of her own and had a ton of friends and family who cared for and supported her. I have to remind myself that I can't know what will happen one way or the other, whether I have children of my own or not.

It's very difficult for women to avoid wrapping up their identity with their ability or inability to be mothers. There's so much pressure on us. Especially today, *mother* is a label that gets people in trouble when they attach it to their self-worth. I see women having children all the time for reasons more connected to their self-worth than to a desire to be parents. Typically, they don't want to be ostracized in society; they want to make sure they are seen and heard in a particular community. They feel that's more of a guarantee if they have children.

What's the difference between a label and your identity? To me, identity is biological and geographical. It's what you were made of, where you come from, what you look like, and how you choose to be identified. At the beginning of each *Blended* episode, I ask everybody to identify themselves—to tell us who they are, what they do, and how they identify. (People share as little or as much as they like.) I do this specifically because much of identity is visual. Since listeners can't see that on a podcast, I want it disclosed.

I'm a Caucasian heterosexual female in my forties with two bonus children and two dogs. I live part-time in Florida, but I am Canadian. My family is from England. That's my identity.

Labels are different. *I'm a runner. I make pottery. I like rock shows.* Those are labels. Labels change. That's why it's problematic to connect them to your self-worth. That said, it's also problematic to connect your identity to self-worth. Uncoupling self-worth from your labels and identity can be challenging. It requires hard work, awareness, and a willingness to have hard conversations with yourself. We all have inherent biases we can't control. But you can always control your reaction.

> **WE CAN'T BE ALL THE LABELS THAT GET PUT ON US AND THAT WE PUT ON OURSELVES.**

It's natural to feel bad about yourself after losing a label or questioning part of your identity. But you can learn how to communicate and respond in a way that mitigates the situation rather than perpetuates it. When you do, you'll always walk away feeling better about yourself. We can't be all the labels that get put on us and that we put on ourselves. That's OK. And then, of course, there are plenty of things about ourselves we can't change. So at the end of the day, you really don't want your self-worth to be based on what other people think of you.

Certainly that's easier said than done. I hated mopping floors. I was fine with answering phones, running retail sales transactions, and even dealing with rude people. But for some reason, the mopping cut me off at the knees. I'd ask myself, *I'm thirty-eight years old—how am I still mopping floors?* Often, mid-task, I played the blame game: blaming the forces that put me in this situation, blaming myself. I usually waited to mop until the place was empty because I didn't want anyone seeing me. There were days when I felt grateful for the job and thought, *If the worst thing I have to do is mop, then I'm doing all right.* There were other days when I felt I simply couldn't do it.

It took me a few months to untangle it from self-worth. I certainly struggled with my ego but ultimately came to understand that I was no less a person mopping floors then I had been six months ago as a director. If people came in while I was mopping, I would put it away immediately, walk right to the desk, and try to distract them with sparkling conversation. But ultimately, I don't think anyone cared. It was more of a me thing than a them thing.

When you lose a label, you're still the same person. If you have to take on work or other labels that you feel are quote-unquote beneath you, try not to let it affect your self-worth. Whenever I'd get down about mopping floors, I'd remind myself that I was doing it so I could work on my business, so I could go speak on stages. By the time I was speaking in front of 2,500 people, I was still a receptionist at a tennis club. I didn't talk about that much. I was playing two different roles and keeping them separate. But it's all part of my story, my journey.

Do the things you have to do in order to do the things you want to do. Labels are just labels. The only reason they ever have emotion behind them—guilt, shame, or whatever—is because we assign that. A label is never a living thing. Whether it's one you like or don't like, try not to attach too much importance to it.

And if you're having trouble finding self-worth outside of your labels, just make up new ones that do give you purpose or pride. That's a hack from the entrepreneur's bag: *assign yourself new labels*. Base them on your hobbies. Or just have fun with it. For example, I was the head of the tennis club. The director of fundraising. I was the director of customer service as well. Occasionally, I was the director of cleanliness. I definitely directed that mop where to go.

IDENTITY AND LABELS ARE *MEANT* TO CHANGE.

Whatever you tell yourself, don't let other people control your self-esteem. Your identity is what you make it. It doesn't derive from a label or how other people think you should live. And identity can change. How you identify today may not be how you identify later. So enjoy the process. Identity and labels are *meant* to change—so get used to it.

One thing you can't avoid is the inevitability of losing a certain amount of friends when a label is taken away from you. Then again, that's how you figure out who you want in your life—and who you want to be when the label stripping happens to someone else. But when you remove the *impact* of someone else's opinion, you also remove the power that those labels have over you.

Shake them off. Live your best life. Be proud of who you are. And stand in your own truth.

CHAPTER 11

YOU CAN CHOOSE GRACE OVER GRIT

I ONCE READ THAT SCORPIOS TEND TO RUMINATE AND punish themselves. So that's my excuse. What's yours?

We all do it in a hundred different ways. I constantly second-guess myself. Do you ever ask yourself, *Did I hurt someone's feelings? Did my voice have a negative tone? Did somebody take something I said the wrong way and it ruined their day, when really they are doing a good job for us and working hard and I want to acknowledge and appreciate that, but at the same time I need to hold them accountable for things, and that's challenging as a leader and entrepreneur within the delicate balance of having empathy but at the same time needing to ensure people do what they say they're going to do in order to move your business forward?* You get it.

Sometimes I think about these things hours after the fact. Other times I think about them all night. Sometimes it lasts for days.

I once had a freelancer named Mallory, who worked for me

about five to ten hours a week. She was OK. She was one of my virtual assistants, and I had even recommended her to a couple of other people. But she started making mistakes on a few things, and consistently, so I moved those tasks over to a different freelancer. Eventually, her hours went down to only a couple a week. She asked if there was more work.

After thinking about it, I went back to her and said, "There's really not much more work I can give you. It sounds like this is where we should probably part ways." Mallory said OK, no problem, blah blah blah. Then she sent me a letter saying I owed her sixty days of pay.

I told her I would of course pay her for the days she worked and to please invoice me for them in the way she always had but that I thought we should move on at that point. Next, although she had told me she'd worked four hours since our last invoice, she charged me for 6 1/2 hours. And I was like, *Fine, I'll just pay her the 6 1/2 hours and be done with it.*

But then she and another former virtual assistant of mine started sending harassing letters, accusing me of owing her $800. I answered a couple of times explaining that I had paid all invoices. Mallory kept saying, "I want my $800." So I blocked her email. Then she logged into my email account so she could forward me an email from my own account. When I didn't answer that one, she logged into my website and deleted a few webpages.

When I didn't answer still, she drove her son to my house while I was in the middle of a live show so he could knock on the door and disrupt the show knowing full well I had dogs that would bark when the doorbell rang. Then she tried to take me to small claims court for $600, which made no sense to me. Not only did she lower the number, but there's a fee to start a small claim. What was the point when she would've had to pay $175 to the court? Why not try to get $1,000 out of me? I thought, *What is even happening here?*

So I countersued for fourteen grand: for the missing website pages, her hacking into my email, and all the lost time of dealing with the situation. The main reason I chose such a high number was to deter her from repeating the behavior. I had horrible visions of her doing this to another woman who owned a business, had never been sued before, and would have to spend money she didn't have—not on her business but to fight something like this in small claims court.

The next step was Zoom court with a judge. It did not go as expected. The judge seemed to side with her. When he asked what she would walk away with, she said $300. He asked me the same thing, and I said $2,500. He then asked if she would pay me $2,200. She said no. So it was time to get ready for court.

Then he asked how many witnesses we had. She had one, that other former virtual assistant of mine. I had three, including my operations manager. The judge said he would be in touch with a date. But then I asked a friend of mine to reach out to Mallory because she had never accepted the payment I'd sent her for the 6 1/2 hours, and I thought that was strange. My friend told her that I believe people should get paid for the work they do, and I would be willing to resend that payment in order for us to call it a day. She accepted it. She went through all of that drama for $150 that had already been paid to her anyway.

Even though I knew I was mostly in the right...even though it seemed like this was a situation where I didn't completely understand the motive or reasoning behind it...I ruminated about this for weeks and weeks. *Maybe I should just pay her for the 60 days. Maybe I am in the wrong.* Or, *What did I do to deserve this treatment?* Or, *How horrible of a person am I for someone to think it's OK to log into my email and website without my permission?*

Eventually, I reaffirmed to myself that it is not OK for someone to use my email and make changes to my website. In the middle of the rumination, I learned my lesson and put a plan in place with my team to offboard someone more properly moving forward.

Maybe it's because of my experiences being bullied, but my first inkling is almost always to assume I'm the problem and then wonder what I could've said or done differently. This is especially true now that I'm a leader. With this freelancer, I asked myself if maybe, back when I let her go, I should've helped her get another job. But of course, if I had, and she'd started making the same kinds of mistakes in the new gig, that would have reflected badly on me. Then, when she brought in the other former assistant of mine, I started reliving my relationship with *her*. Had I treated *her* badly? And then, of course, how stupid could I have been not to change my passwords after letting her go?!

I would obsess on the topic for three or four hours a day. It was brutal. It all happened in my head or the occasional morning spent talking to myself in the bathroom while getting ready for the day. It wasn't affecting my ability to work, but it certainly took up time and space that I could have instead focused on positive aspects of my life. About a year ago, I realized that what I was doing is called *rumination*. I still do it. I'm learning how to manage it.

RUMINATION IS JUST A STORY YOU TELL YOURSELF, ONE THAT MAKES YOU FEEL BETTER OR ABSOLVES YOU OF GUILT.

Rumination is often just a story you tell yourself, one that makes you feel better or absolves you of guilt. You might tell yourself all the nice things you've done for a person who treated you badly and then ask yourself, *How can they treat me like this after all I've done?* The next step might be to generate a long list of actions taken in your life that generally prove you're not a bad person. It can be even more effective to write a letter to that person (without judgment on them or yourself) and then burn it. That kind of rumination serves a purpose: to tell your side of the story when the other person won't listen or without getting into a heated confrontation. Often, we ruminate because we want some kind of acknowledgment from the other person.

I have gotten better about catching myself during a rumination. For example, if I wake up in the middle of the night—maybe the dog jumps off the bed—my brain immediately goes to something negative, and I have a hard time getting back to sleep. Those are usually signs that I'm stuck in my head, overfocusing on something negative. Then I'll try to focus on something positive or do a little gratitude practice. It can be hard to break a rumination, though, because often we tell ourselves we're focusing on it in an effort to learn from whatever the interaction was. We think it's self-improvement.

But rumination is never positive. Everything in life is about balance. And two things can be true at the same time. Self-improvement is important to growth—but obsessive rumination that focuses on the negative will cancel out other improvements. Awareness is key. Anyway, we can get addicted to self-improvement, even after reaching a point of diminishing returns, it could be a kind of obsession. Of course, we should always be working on ourselves and learning from mistakes, but part of self-worth is also being OK with not being OK.

My bouts of rumination also come from feeling like an impostor. I definitely still get imposter syndrome. I worry after a speaking engagement if I feel that I didn't give them exactly what they needed. I feel it every time I win an award. I fought it the whole time I was writing this book, when I was racked by thoughts like, *Who do I think I am to write a book about self-worth? I'm not a self-worth expert! Why would anyone read it or listen to me?* Anytime I feel vulnerable, the imposter creeps in.

It doesn't have to define you. Sometimes the trick is simply awareness. When you catch yourself ruminating, just acknowledge you're doing it. Plus, when you're aware of something, you can communicate it to other people. When you understand your behavior and what triggers it, that's a huge leap forward on the path to self-worth because it keeps your ruminations from escalating into additional drama and trauma toward other people in your life.

I only recently learned how to catch myself. It started when I was going through some stuff with my family, and my therapist said, "You're obsessed." It hit me like a ton of bricks. I thought, *Holy shit, I am obsessed. I wake up thinking about it. I think about it when I brush my teeth.*

When I heard the word *obsessed*, I saw the rumination, and I wanted to learn how to make it stop. Now, if I catch myself ruminating, I tell myself I just need to let it pass through, and I give myself some time and space for that. I'll say to myself over and over, *This too shall pass.*

YOU'RE ALLOWED TO BE A BIT EMOTIONAL.

Rumination is just the result of feeling an emotion that gets stuck inside you and can't move around. You just need to help it move through. You can't gaslight yourself and say, "Be happy right now!" You're allowed to be a bit emotional. Life sometimes can be hard. Tell your loved ones that you're going to disappear for a while and read a book or whatever.

Still, that kind of stress can have serious physiological ramifications. Everyone handles stress and anxiety differently. But understanding rumination and increasing your awareness of it can be steps toward alleviating some of the stress and anxiety we feel around emotional experiences that can otherwise be debilitating.

Boundaries can help. I've discussed them several times in this book—they're that important and also the hardest part of the journey to self-worth. Everyone seems OK with boundaries when we talk about them in general, but implementing a specific one is very difficult. Often, when we put up one or try to, it blows up in our faces. You have to be extremely confident about whatever boundary you're instituting, and you have to repeat it over and over, not just for yourself but for the other person. Remind them why it's there and why it's important. People will knock them down, and you will have the wind taken out of you, and you will wonder, *If this is so hard, maybe I shouldn't do it.*

Even with boundaries, we still tend to define ourselves by what other people say about us. That means that some days we feel like good people and some days monsters. These are labels you can ditch. We don't have to define ourselves. It's OK to one day feel like a superhero and the next day worry about saying the wrong thing to someone. Neither of those circumstances makes you a good or bad person.

Maybe instead of trying to define ourselves, we can try to define our core values. And then, whenever we don't know who we are or are relying too much on other people's opinions of us, we can return to those values. Therapists can be excellent guides in this kind of work. You can also get help from books. Just remember that sometimes the values you hold in your twenties will be different than those in your thirties and those in your forties.

Anyway, rumination and a failure to set boundaries are often just forms of self-punishment. And punishing yourself is antithetical to self-worth. Yet we do it all the time. Some of the ways I've punished myself include picking my lip and biting the skin around my nails. I told you about this earlier. When do I do it? When obsessing over something negative.

With some introspection and retrospection, I've come to believe I do that because it makes me uglier. It deforms me in some way. Whatever I'm ruminating over causes me to subconsciously punish myself. I've quit biting my lip, but I still chew my nails and the skin around them. It hurts. Sometimes, I cause them to bleed. Who is that helping? I'm working on it.

Think about it: we don't really ruminate on things that go well. Sometimes we don't even celebrate such wins. Sometimes that's specifically because we're spending so much time obsessing over the negative. It's a vicious cycle of *I'm not good enough.* We miss out on beautiful parts of life when we're stuck in the hamster wheel.

There's one question in particular that keeps us running that wheel. Do you ever catch yourself wondering, *Why is it always me? Why am I the common denominator?* This is another way of blaming ourselves, of thinking there must be something wrong with us and that's why bad things always happen to us. It gives us an excuse to be victims. Maybe we make ourselves the common denominator because we need to matter.

The logical truth is that, if everyone feels they're a common denominator, then no one is. We're all just in our own heads. The only common denominator is the one among all of us: rumination itself.

Like I said, acknowledgment helps. Also, if you can, try to figure out what your triggers are and which life experiences create them. Most important, when you're in a ruminating space, have grace for yourself. And communicate your headspace with those around you so you don't affect them. Recognize that this too shall pass.

My advocacy work also helps me dismantle the hamster wheel. When you're empowering other people, you don't even have time to focus on yourself. Rumination is very self-centered. You won't be able to create safe spaces for others if you're continually in your head and negativity. Therefore, the inverse is true: focusing on other people and helping to empower them can also be a way to break free of rumination (while also empowering others to become aware of rumination).

Back when I was sued by that freelancer, I didn't have many tools in my toolbox. The rumination caused my anxiety to spike, and that definitely affected my behavior in Zoom court. She was very even-keeled and unattached; I was extremely emotional. I think if I had understood rumination at the time and my tendency toward it and the effect it has on me, I could have been much more calm and conversational throughout the whole affair. I remember getting off the Zoom call and feeling pissed. I was yelling all over the place. The drama took up so much emotional and mental space throughout. Even after it was over, I remained emotionally wrapped up in it.

I didn't learn what rumination is, how to recognize it happening, and how to free myself of it until I was forty-four years old. What a long and drawn out period of rumination and self-punishment I could have avoided if I had just read my own book. I had enough grit. If only I had given myself more grace.

THIS ISN'T THE END; IT'S JUST THE BEGINNING

IF YOU'VE MADE IT TO THIS FINAL PAGE, THEN MAYBE, JUST maybe, you see yourself somewhere in my story. In the chaos and clarity. In the striving and the surrender. In the voice that got quiet for too long before learning how to roar again. This journey wasn't about becoming someone new. It was about unbecoming everything I was never meant to be so I could finally see the woman I am.

There were years I chased validation like it was oxygen. I wore productivity like armor and achievements like proof that I mattered. I measured my worth in who I could impress, what I could produce, and how well I could hide the fear that I might not be enough.

YOUR WORTH IS NOT SOMETHING YOU EARN; IT'S SOMETHING YOU REMEMBER.

But here's the truth I found through heartbreaks, reinventions, audacious pivots, and coffee-fueled clarity: your worth is not something you earn; it's something you remember. Once you remember it, once you *really* see it, everything begins to change. The moment you stop waiting to be chosen is the moment you realize you were the one you were waiting for all along.

Remember the grandmother I lived with in Vancouver? On her deathbed, I told her I forgave her. I wanted her to go with peace. By that time, I had come to learn that, however cruel and dismissive she had been to me, it actually had nothing to do with me. She was dealing with her own trauma. I think she was probably not happy with herself. I can't know for sure—like I said before, I didn't ask.

I have been on a journey to understand more about my generational trauma and what needs healing. Sometimes how we feel about ourselves can be passed down through the generations; how we treat each other as family comes from that generational trauma. I have seen it play out throughout my life in a variety of ways, the feelings of inadequacy, the anger. Those are definitely things my mom and grandmother have felt. People in my family have been struggling with their self-worth for centuries.

Eventually, I decided that wouldn't be me or my life. I've made a conscious choice to stop the cycle. Sure, I don't have kids of my own. But there's more than that to ending generational trauma. You can also heal family trauma backward, moving up the line. And so I forgave my grandmother. She didn't say much. But she didn't seem angry. She knew what I was talking about. And I think my gesture brought her some peace.

Generational healing is a huge part of the journey toward self-worth. It certainly has been for me. That's why it stops now, stops with me. Each of us has the power and responsibility to break that cycle.

The work I've done to develop self-worth, to discover and act on my superpower, and even to write this book will hopefully translate to generational healing within my community so we can all heal in our own ways. That's one of the reasons I do what I do. Now that you have read this book, is it any wonder I've dedicated my career to giving people space to feel seen and heard? The stories in here are most often of times I felt invisible or unappreciated: not being taken seriously at my parents' company, the childhood bullying, being kicked to the curb by my first fiancé, being taken advantage of by Bonnie and my former freelancer assistant. Those are all examples of me not being seen. I hope, in these pages and in my stories, you have yourself felt seen and heard, and have begun to walk or at least envision your own path toward self-worth.

Sharing our stories with one another can change lives. During Lipedema Awareness Month in 2025, I posted publicly about my condition on LinkedIn. Shortly thereafter, I received a direct message thanking me because my post had been a light-bulb moment for her. She told me she looked up the condition and is now convinced she has it, that everything I shared lines up with her personal experience: the weight, pain and tenderness, the bruising. We messaged back-and-forth all afternoon so I could share resources and advice. It ended up being a big day for her, and I felt so happy and excited for her.

It's your turn. This book might have been about my story, but the next chapter is yours.

What dream have you silenced because someone told you it was "too much"? What truth have you buried to make others comfortable? What would happen if you finally gave yourself full permission to be you?

**START MESSY. START SCARED.
START ANYWAY. JUST START.**

Today, not some day, is the moment you get to choose yourself. Loudly, unapologetically, and wholeheartedly. Start messy. Start scared. Start anyway. Just start.

Actually, my next book is yours too: I'm dedicating it to how women feel about themselves. I want us to understand a little more about how we show up in the world, think about ourselves, and affect each other. Imagine how much faster we can reach gender parity if we know all of that about one another! This book told stories from my life experiences. My intention for the next one is to elevate other voices.

Meanwhile, remember to celebrate the wins. Don't wait for other people to big you up; you've got to big yourself up. You don't want to look back and not remember all that you accomplished simply because you didn't take a moment to celebrate them.

And trust that when you're walking the path of self-worth and you're comfortable with its ebbs and flows, your superpower will come to you, and you can start piecing together a life that impacts others and your own journey with self-worth.

I haven't reached any kind of destination. There are still days when I am overwhelmed by the feeling of not being good enough. It's like an invisible hood that covers me and makes me want to check out. In those moments, I accept the feeling without succumbing to it. I go for a walk, change my environment, or say my affirmation. I try to find a way to get out of my head. Writing this book has also been a way to get out of my head, to pull experiences from my life and share them in these pages.

Our experiences teach us, but they do not define us. We are not broken. We are becoming. And our becoming is beautiful.

Now, go—take up space, speak your truth, find your superpower, and own your worth like it's your birthright. Because it is. And always has been.

To our success,
Sarah

Sarah

ACKNOWLEDGMENTS

I WANT TO ACKNOWLEDGE AND APPRECIATE EVERYONE WHO challenged me, championed me, or cheered from the sidelines. This book carries your fingerprints.

I want to acknowledge and appreciate my editor, who refused to let me stay on the surface and demanded truth, depth, and the kind of vulnerability I thought I wasn't ready for. Thank you for holding me to the standard I didn't know I needed.

I want to acknowledge and appreciate my publishers. Your guidance, patience, and belief in this project helped breathe life into every page. I never felt like I was doing this alone.

I want to acknowledge and appreciate my team: you reminded me who I was every time imposter syndrome crept in with its tired little voice. Your faith in me was louder, and I'm so grateful for that.

I want to acknowledge and appreciate the incredible humans who contributed support. Thank you for your words, your energy, and your endorsement. You helped me feel seen.

I want to acknowledge and appreciate Oprah. You don't know me, but your legacy and presence have inspired this work and my company more than you could imagine. Your truth-telling, boundary-breaking brilliance is stitched into every chapter of not only this book but every chapter of building my legacy.

I want to acknowledge and appreciate the supply-chain community for all of its support: the followers who engaged and sent me messages of encouragement and all who will support me again by buying the book or attending a live shows or events.

Finally, I want to acknowledge and appreciate my husband—the steady hand, the soft place, the rock. You've been everything I needed, even when I didn't know how to ask for it. Thank you for holding space for this version of me to emerge.

ABOUT THE AUTHOR

SARAH BARNES-HUMPHREY is a globally recognized storyteller, podcast host, and fierce advocate for self-worth and authentic leadership. The founder and voice behind *Let's Talk Supply Chain*, the Women in Supply Chain series, and *Blended Podcast*, Sarah has built a powerful platform to amplify voices that often go unheard. Her work—featured by BBC World News, Bloomberg, *Inc.*, *The New Yorker,* and *HuffPost*—centers on creating spaces where vulnerability sparks transformation. With a passionate global following, Sarah brings courage, clarity, and connection to everything she does. A proud Canadian and stepmom, Sarah finds peace with sand beneath her feet, the ocean in her ears, and community at her core.

www.ingramcontent.com/pod-product-compliance
Lightning Source LLC
Chambersburg PA
CBHW030525080526
44586CB00011B/329